PROCLAIMING

THE

SCANDAL

Christian Mission and Modern Culture

EDITED BY
ALAN NEELY, H. WAYNE PIPKIN,
AND WILBERT R. SHENK

In the Series:

PROCLAIMING

THE

SCANDAL

REFLECTIONS ON
POSTMODERN MINISTRY

JEROME E. BURCE

TRINITY PRESS
INTERNATIONAL
HARRISBURG, PENNSYLVANIA

Trinity Press International, P.O. Box 1321, Harrisburg, PA 17105

Trinity Press International is a division of the Morehouse Group.

Library of Congress Cataloging-in-Publication Data

Burce, Jerome E.
    Proclaiming the scandal : reflections on postmodern ministry / Jerome E. Burce.
        p. cm. — (Christian mission and modern culture)
    ISBN 1-56338-332-2 (pbk. : alk. paper)
    1. Evangelistic work.   2. Pastoral theology.   I. Series.

    BV3793 .B87 2000
    269—dc21   00–041788

Printed in the United States of America

00 01 02 03 04 05   10 9 8 7 6 5 4 3 2 1

Contents

Preface to the Series

Both Christian mission and modern culture, widely regarded as antagonists, are in crisis. The emergence of the modern mission movement in the early nineteenth century cannot be understood apart from the rise of technocratic society. Now, at the beginning of the twenty-first century, both modern culture and Christian mission face an uncertain future.

One of the developments integral to modernity was the way the role of religion in culture was redefined. Whereas religion had played an authoritative role in the culture of Christendom, modern culture was highly critical of religion and increasingly secular in its assumptions. A sustained effort was made to banish religion to the backwaters of modern culture.

The decade of the 1980s witnessed further momentous developments on the geopolitical front with the collapse of communism. In the aftermath of the breakup of the system of power blocs that dominated international relations for a generation, it is clear that religion has survived even if its institutionalization has undergone deep change and its future forms are unclear. Secularism continues to oppose religion, while technology has emerged as a major source of power and authority in modern culture. Both confront Christian faith with fundamental questions.

The purpose of this series is to probe these developments from a variety of angles with a view to helping the church understand its missional responsibility to a culture in crisis. One important resource is the church's experience of two centuries of cross-cultural mission that has reshaped the church into a global Christian *ecumene*. The focus of our inquiry will be the church in modern culture. The series (1) examines modern/postmodern culture from a missional point of view; (2) develops the theological agenda that the church in modern culture must address in order to recover its own integrity; and (3) tests fresh conceptualizations of the nature and mission of the church as it engages modern culture. In other words, these volumes are intended to be a forum where conventional assumptions can be challenged and alternative formulations explored.

This series is a project authorized by the Institute of Mennonite Studies, research agency of the Associated Mennonite Biblical Seminary, and supported by a generous grant from the Pew Charitable Trusts.

1

The Gospel as Scandal

The Premise

Cleveland, Ohio. Second Week of Easter, 1999, in the waning days of a parish pastor's post-Holy Week hiatus—

Ever so slowly the dam softens, and words, seeping fitfully through crevices of synapse and neuron, wire and pixel, begin their altogether wondrous appearance on the computer screen before me. "Indwelling" them as we do, we forget what little marvels they are: words, that is; sounds compounded and strung together in complexities of rhyme and reason that make the decorative intricacies of the baroque appear, by contrast, as little more than the wall scratchings of a cavedwelling primitive.[1] Yet the greater marvel is not their form but their effect. Incessantly creative, words give form and shape and also substance to the worlds we inhabit, both for good and ill, as the linguistic philosophers have been at pains to teach us, though we whose worlds have been shaped in significant part by the first chapters of Genesis and John should not have needed the instruction. Words make "what is." They also make "what is not." Words of God do this in the first place. Thereafter so do the words that proceed from the mouths of the human creatures God formed "in our image, after our likeness."

1

Oddly, the satanic twisting of that image to which all of us have been subjected does not, like the cutting of Samson's hair, steal the power from what we say. It merely perverts it, with the consequence that we are all obliged as human beings to discover at some point—sooner more often than later—that while sticks and stones may break our bones, words will *surely* hurt us. This, of course, is what the playground chant is really all about. One of the enduring lessons of the past bitter, violent century is that false words in the mouths of grossly evil men are greatly to be feared, possessing as they do a strength not only hideous, but also enormous, enough to call into obscene being a reality like Buchenwald.

Be it also said and acknowledged after the past century that for all the words that maim and kill there are "counterwords" abroad in the world that heal and make alive. Of these, to be sure, there have always been some—the universal "there, there" of the mother's soothing croon, again the occasional flight of poetic rhapsody or Churchillian rhetoric, each in its own way invested with an amazing power to revive drooping flesh. Yet something greater by far than these is also among us, as indeed it has been ever since that day of grace when the Word saw fit to take on this same drooping flesh and pitch his tent among us, eventually occupying every bed that drooping flesh is bound to lie in, from cradle to grave. Being "risen indeed," as the Church[2] shouts in its annual trumpeting of Easter, this same Word continues even now to oversee the uttering of words, his words, the effect of which is to transform twisted images of God into his own "word made flesh full of grace and truth" likeness.

Those so transformed are simultaneously author-ized—literally, turned into authors—and hurled into the world as freshly minted makers of a scarcely conceivable new creation, each of them equipped with an arsenal of little marvels beyond imagining which, when spoken, can turn something so elusive as peace into "what eternally is," or something so ubiquitous and deadly as sin into "what eternally is not." Or so says the Author-izer in John 20:21–23, the heart of last Sunday's bout with the good news of Jesus Christ— "the Gospel" as we continue by convention to say. Even in its older form, this term seems a strangely tepid locution for the glad tidings of great, outlandish joy that the words of and concerning Jesus ultimately prove to be. In the end, they undo even Buchenwald (Rev 20:13; 21:1–4). Such is the power of these words. Such too is their promise.

Now for the challenge: try telling all this to people in the pews of the typical North American mainline Protestant church. Try telling it, for that matter, to their Roman Catholic or evangelical counterparts.

The Argument

The exhortation of the previous paragraph can be read in two ways, ironically and straightforwardly. Both readings are intended. Each points to one of two sides of the essential argument I plan to make in this essay. Both also bear heavily on the argument's coda, a piece of pastoral encouragement which, all else said and done, is my chief reason for undertaking the labor of writing.

In terse summary: side one of the argument (chapter 2 in particular) asserts that countless hearers of the Gospel in North America are loathe to trust what they are hearing, especially as this Gospel establishes their identity as authorized emissaries of Christ and so gives immediate, compelling definition to their central and common purpose as members of his Church. The loathing runs deep, especially in the churches of the old Protestant mainline. It bears a stamp manifestly peculiar to an immersion in the dominant culture of North America. It begs the painful question whether the Church's purpose is capable of fulfillment by those afflicted with it—the doubting faithful, as I will sometimes be moved to call them.

Side two of the argument (primarily chapter 3) insists that the only reasonable response to this loathing is a cheerful, vivid, sharp, and unrelenting iteration of the very Gospel that its hearers are flinching from. By "reasonable" I mean that which conforms to the command, the example, indeed the very nature of Reason's Source, who happens at one and the same time to be the Gospel's content and the Church's sole excuse for being. I will urge that the question of what the Gospel is and is not requires much closer attention than is commonly given to it on all sides of the North American socioreligious spectrum, right as well as left. Failure to pay this attention is causing the faithful, already burdened with their loathing, to be afflicted still further with proposals for the alleviation of it that are manifestly unreasonable and necessarily destructive of their purpose as Church. On the other hand, where this attention does get paid, there the Church's purpose does get achieved—dependably, in ways dependably surprising (chapter 4).

The coda (also in chapter 4, though heavily anticipated in chapter 1) consists of an invitation to my colleagues in the pastoral ministry of the Church to start trusting this. One might speak of it as side two of the argument reprised and obeyed for the sake of those to whom the Gospel has been preeminently entrusted.

Pastoral Purpose: First Reflection

It is to these, after all, that this essay is chiefly addressed: men and women who, like me, stand in a pulpit or at an altar Sunday after Sunday, charged with both performance and supervision of the public proclamation of the Word of God within one of those variously designated collectivities—parish, congregation, meeting, assembly—whose essence is a more or less weekly gathering of worshipping Christians. One of my many preliminary assumptions is that this act and oversight of proclamation is what pastoral ministry is fundamentally for and about. This assumption, like most of the others I will here and there divulge, is a derived one, its principles imbibed from the Lutheran confessional tradition in which I was raised and schooled, its tried-and-tested character as an operative axiom developed over almost twenty years of theological and pastoral practice within that same tradition. Any more it strikes me as self-evident, a "no-brainer" in the apt locution of a former parishioner.

Noting that the conception of pastoral ministry has, over the past few decades, been as subject as most anything else ecclesiastical to trends and fashions and two-year fads, one is obliged almost immediately to wonder why. After all, amid all the flaring and fizzling of proposals as to what pastor, priest, or minister is supposed to be about, one thing has remained stubbornly constant. Come Sunday morning somebody has had to stand up and preach the sermon, or guide the public prayers, or take responsibility for the content of the chancel drama, or answer hurried questions between services about what the kids are being taught in Sunday School. During the week that same somebody has had to make sure the sick and suffering of the community are being heard (if not answered) as they've wrestled with their questions about God's doing in their lives. She or he has also married and buried, with only the Word to distinguish her services or his from those of the secular official or the articulate family friend. He or she has been the one to whom those on the outside have chiefly looked in their efforts to discern "what this church stands for," and what "this church" stands for is, of course, inextricably and ultimately linked to what "this church" makes of what God has once said or is presently saying.

Pastors at base are tenders of the Word, locally uttered; and this is so, necessarily, even for Roman Catholic pastors of pre–Vatican II sympathies who continue to conceive of their ministry primarily in sacramental terms. What else are sacraments, said Augustine, but visible words, God's grace conveyed in deed and substance to be sure, but always in the company of a spoken, defining declaration as to what the grace in question at this particular moment happens to be. Pastors proclaim. That's what they do. That's what they're paid for, to cite the trenchant if annoying bleat of those impious, penny-pinching old rams who continue as ever to insist on making their presence known at annual business meetings of the flock.

But to say merely that pastors proclaim is not yet to identify the ends to which this proclaiming is directed. Here of late is where no end of confusion has arisen, much more than in so recent a past as my own childhood, which coincided with my father's initial decade of service as a pastor and missionary for the Lutheran Church–Missouri Synod. Those were the dying years of Christendom—the Constantinian era as some also call it, when ancient cultural assumptions arrived at in the fourth century A.D. through a Roman emperor's embrace of the Christian faith could be said still to hold sway in the cultural imagination of North America.[3] Details tell. "Protestant, Catholic or Jew?" asks the U.S. Army of its World War II draftees, giving little if any thought to the possibility that a citizen soldier might worship Allah, or pine for the serenity of a Buddha.

Again, in the introduction to a 1946 edition of Jane Austen's *Pride and Prejudice* by what one takes to be an essentially secular publisher, the editor, musing hypothetically on her selection of a half-dozen books to accompany a long-term exile to a desert island, takes pains to advise the reader that the first chosen would "of course" be the Bible.[4] These days the line startles. Back then, presumably, it soothed. Prevailing pieties were being stroked—of that editor's employer in the first place, and then of those to whom that employer hoped to sell books.

That book-buying public was American, perhaps to some extent also Canadian. To be American or Canadian in the late 1940s and early '50s was to be Christian, except in that rare and decidedly less fortunate circumstance (so thought the majority) under which a citizen might be a Jew. Even then it was generally expected, also at the highest levels of the cultural establishment, that all good citizens should in some fashion or another fear God and attend to His Word, if not by appearing regularly at church or synagogue then at least by reading and knowing the Bible. Such atheistic scoffers as stalked the land did so as lapsed Christians, or nonpracticing Jews. To be neither Christian nor Jew (if only by heritage) was quite Un-American, no doubt also Un-Canadian. People of that ilk, known otherwise as the heathen, were to be found between the Atlantic and Pacific coasts only in urban Chinatowns, or perhaps on Indian reservations. Otherwise one sought them out overseas, in strange and exotic lands like India or New Guinea, the one to which my parents were sent in 1948.

Christendom, the writers assure us, had its disadvantages. A lack of clarity about pastoral purpose was not one of them. Came a day in that year of our Lord, 1948, when my father found himself suddenly disgorged from the bowels of a biplane onto a freshly carved airstrip in New Guinea's mountainous hinterland. As he stood there collecting his wits he no doubt suffered his share of the standard newcomer's apprehensions. Those apprehensions, however, could not have been mixed with doubts or qualms as to *why* he was there. Crudely phrased, he had come to make Christians of non-Christians. In embarking on this project he knew he could count on broad support among kith, kindred, and fellow believers "back home," where great swathes of the citizenry, not only Lutheran, were still singing *From Greenland's Icy Mountains* (the unaltered version) with gusto and nary a hint of embarrassment. I should think he found this psychologically useful, perhaps sustaining, as he trudged through the rain and mud toward his first night's lodging.

Much the same comfort was available that year to almost all other graduates of North American seminaries,

the vast majority of whom found themselves being similarly disgorged, albeit from train or automobile, into the
cities, towns, or hamlets of their first call. The pay might be
abysmal, and it often was. The compensating rewards of
warm welcome and instant respect were inversely substantial. The local populace would be well aware of what the
new pastor had come to do. Sectarian rivalries notwithstanding, it could also be counted on generally to encourage his doing of it. He would likely pick up where the old
pastor had left off, slogging away with fresh and youthful
energy at the perennial project of making good Christians
of bad ones and better Christians of good ones. If
Protestant he would do this by preaching and teaching the
Bible; if Catholic by hearing confessions and presiding at
Mass. He would also do it by overseeing the rites of passage;
by seeking out the lapsed; by encouraging good works, both
personal and societal; by safeguarding morals, public as
well as private; by warning from time to time against god-
less and ipso facto un-American ideologies like
Communism. If worth his salt he would be acutely sensi-
tive to the hypocrisy that any establishment of
Christianity, *de facto* no less than *de iure*, will entail. He
would therefore assume a position in that long and noble
line of pastors reaching back to Chrysostom and beyond
who have made it their prophetic business to annoy
Christian society with a grating insistence that Christ,
intent as he is on new creation, does not take kindly to
veneers of idle religiosity. And even in this, as in all his
doing, he could reasonably expect to enjoy the public's
fundamental esteem as one who served both God and
country, the latter by stiffening the moral and spiritual
fiber on which the commonweal depended, the former by
engendering faith and obedience in the baptized and
preparing them to survive the final judgment. An older
colleague, educated in the early '50s, tells me that the
point and purpose of pastoral ministry was not a topic of

debate or even much conversation in his years at the seminary. Looking back one fails to see a reason why it should have been.

Two decades later, as I was entering the seminary, it was starting to be. By now it necessarily is. In 1999 a newly graduated seminarian, intending to spend the next several years of her life evangelizing Mongolian herders, will not think to garner approving smiles at the passport office when she reveals the purpose of her application. She will know better. As a daughter of the much maligned "religious right"—who but the religious right undertakes such projects these days—she has long since learned that her passions and purposes annoy her neighbors. On the exceedingly slim chance that the seminary she just graduated from was a mainline divinity school, this lesson has been pounded home by the frowns and icy shoulders of classmates with whom she made the mistake of divulging her plans. For their part those same classmates, now renting moving vans, are doing so with much higher anxiety than their forebears knew. The pay in Buzzard's Beak, Montana, is still abysmal. The debt this pay is obliged to assuage is massively larger. The welcoming committee at journey's end will be smaller and quieter, much less inclusive of the broader community. Worse still, or maybe worst of all, the goal of the journey is grievously less clear and compelling than it used to be.

A likely scenario, all too easily imagined: the good, graying people of Third Church, Buzzard's Beak have made it known they want a minister. When pressed to say precisely why, they've stumbled and stuttered. Precisely here is where the discussion at the pre-call interview became especially frustrating. Ministerial duties were enumerated, to be sure. The points and purposes of those duties were not, except in strictly functional terms. "We want our church to grow," they said, except for one or two, recent attendees at a wider church assembly, who trotted out their sudden grasp of mid-to-late '90s ecclesiastical newspeak and turned wish into onerous demand. "We want *you* to grow our church." To what recognizably Christian end did they want this? They did not say. As I will later argue, they did not say it because they could not say it.

And therein lies the greater burden that now weighs on our young graduate as he crawls behind the wheel of his van. From now on it rests with him, almost solely with him, he feels, to articulate a sufficient reason for embracing the comparative isolation, drudgery, and poverty of a small town pastor's "lifestyle," as we've come to call it. He guesses the day will come, too soon, when a bright, teen-aged son, chafing at the restrictions his father's vocational choice has imposed on him, will wonder plaintively why bright Dad became a minister and not a lawyer, or an equally well-paid psychologist, perhaps. Even now his tired, nervous spouse is poking edgily at him with much the same question.

Mulling on these things, our graduate turns the key, and the thought strikes like a knife. If going to Mongolia to make Christians of non-Christians is these days an illegitimate project—so books and teachers have told him; so he in turn has told his classmate—then going to Montana to make good Christians of bad ones is at best a dubious project. Moreover, if the evangelizing of Mongolian herders is now an act of egregious arrogance, of indefensible Christian imperialism, then so is the evangelizing of that ever-increasing crop of non-Christians who herd sheep or in whatever other fashion carve out a living for themselves in Montana. But if this be the case, then how in heaven's name is he to "grow" that church?

Pew-Level Notes on a Cultural Revolution

In seeking to characterize this generational shift in pastoral expectation, intent, and sense of purpose, one gropes for words adequate to the task. "Dramatic," leaping to mind, seems somehow to underplay the matter. Larger words are also needed when one attempts to account for it, as I now do, very broadly.

Sometime during these past fifty years there came to North America a revolution, or a Great Disruption, as Francis Fukuyama is presently calling it.[5] Said simply, in terms applicable to the present argument, Christendom has fallen, breathtakingly, with seeming finality, like Humpty Dumpty tumbling from his wall, nevermore to be reassembled however many of the king's horses and men may by moved to have a crack at it. Again details tell. In early summer, 1999, the Cleveland *Plain Dealer* reports that the commander at a U.S. Army base somewhere in the southern part of the country has taken steps to accommodate the ritualistic preferences of his Wiccan soldiers, and is studiously ignoring the offended cries of conservative ministers in the surrounding community. Or this: my own immediate editor, a Microsoft Word 7.0 spell checker, insists on flagging Deuteronomy and Thessalonians as misspellings. One concludes, not unfairly, that the tribe and culture of which Bill Gates is symbolic chief knows not the Bible, nor does it especially care that others do.

It is not my purpose here to chronicle the revolution or to account for why it happened. Nor would I dare to. Doctoral candidates, I imagine, will still be writing dissertations on the subject many years hence. In the meantime certain brave observers have been doing their best amid the swirl of its unfolding to give the rest of us a conceptual grasp of what has seemed to be going on. One thinks of Harvey Cox and Langdon Gilkey, of Peter Berger and Richard John Neuhaus.[6] Their task in retrospect has been thankless and in large part futile, their excellent analyses all too rapidly confounded by the onrush of trends and events, especially over the past decade. The city today is not secular, the public square no longer naked. Rumors of angels blossomed five years ago into a fevered fascination with angels that lingers still. God may yet be seriously up for grabs, but He/She/It is most certainly not dead, not in the imagination of the public at large nor even in the mind of the public that thinks. This last item, by the way, must surely come as the largest surprise to those who steadfastly predicted other outcomes thirty years ago. Harvey Cox could not then have imagined that the *New Republic* would be adding a Jean Bethke Elshtain to its masthead in 1998. He would not then have dared to dream that he himself would be publishing theological analyses in the *Atlantic* in 1999.[7]

Religion, in other words, is not passé in America, anything but. Christendom has fallen even so. To put the matter precisely: what the revolution of the past decades has accomplished, inarguably, is to remove Jesus Christ as an inevitable ingredient in the dominant North American description of the divine—even among Christians.

Working pastors know this. They are constantly gleaning this knowledge not only from the stuff of popular culture but, more critically, from the conversation of the devoted laity. Four years ago the systematician Carl E. Braaten complained in an essay addressed to other theological professionals that Christocentrism had given way among them to theocentrism, again that too many were reducing Christology to a thin, unorthodox gruel of "Jesuology."[8] Braaten might just as well have directed his plaint to the 5.7 million members of his own Evangelical Lutheran Church in America. In a 1997 survey entitled "Lutheran Beliefs and Practices," the fraternal organization Lutheran Brotherhood discovered, among innumerable other things, that 67 percent of respondents agreed with the statement that "although there are many religions in the world, most of them lead to the same God." Sixty percent concurred that "the main purpose of the gospel is God's rules for right living." Finding also that 66 percent disagreed that "salvation is received only by those who believe in Christ," one wants to conclude that the large majority of

Lutherans understood those all-important "rules for right living" to be readily available in 1997 in venues other than Christianity—in secular, irreligious venues as well, one assumes, certainly for the 56 percent who affirmed that "God is satisfied if a person lives the best life one can."

This, obviously, is not the stuff of robust, meat-and-potatoes Christology. There is here no necessary, essential connection between the terms "Christ" and "God." There is also here a manifest disconnection between the terms "Christ" and "salvation." St. Paul would not be amused, as Braaten elsewhere points out with characteristic vigor.[9] Neither would Luther, as another Lutheran systematician, Edward H. Schroeder, underscores in an essay devoted specifically to the Lutheran Brotherhood survey.[10]

Equally unamused, I assert, would have been the Lutheran generation of post–World War II adults, guided as they were by pastors who insisted that Luther's Small Catechism and snippets of the Pauline epistles (among one hundred or more other Bible verses) be ingested and thoroughly memorized as a prerequisite to confirmation and admission to the Lord's Table. They were Christian "exclusivists," these grandparents of ours, though they would not readily have grasped the term, it being ours, not theirs. Acts 4:12, the apostolic declaration that people are saved by no name under heaven other than Christ's, did not dismay them. They did not think of it as a scandalous word, a word too much like the dominical description of divorce in Mark 10—difficult, that is; demanding of a culturally acceptable explanation. Instead they received it. They more or less trusted it as *ipsissimum verbum Dei*. They also obeyed it, hearing it in conjunction with Matthew 28 as a call to missionary arms, said arms to be wielded almost exclusively overseas. Back home they could take comfort in the thought that however much one's preacher might rant about "papist error" and the eschatalogical implications thereof, even so the nice Catholic family across the street surely knew enough about Christ to allow one to entertain kindly hopes for them—perhaps even enough to allow one's daughter to marry their son without having to fear for the eternal destiny of the grandchildren. Acts 4:12, in other words, made for fairly easy believing.

Not so now. Said grandchildren, duly raised Lutheran or Catholic and presently verging on grandparenthood themselves, confront a quite different postrevolutionary reality as they look across their own street. Chances are the nice family that's been living over there for the past twenty years doesn't go to church at all. Their son, the boy one's daughter flirted with and later married, has not been baptized and has long since made it plain that he will not be. Daughter herself checks in at church on Christmas and Easter, but never more often than that. Three months from now the first baby is due. Daughter thus far has breathed nary a word about having it baptized, or dedicated, for that matter. Grandma-and-Grandpa-to-be are not broaching the subject. They fear a family uproar. Grasping for comfort, they seize hold of the hollow mantras of the day, the slogans of the Lutheran Brotherhood survey featured prominently among them: that all religions lead to the same god; that this god contents god's easily satisfied self with our best efforts to be good; that the goodness this one-and-same god looks for is a relative and ambiguous thing, so that what is good, let's say, for one father (e.g., that he take his children to church on Sunday morning) may be different but certainly no more valid than what is good for another father (e.g., that he take his children to their soccer matches on Sunday morning). In seizing on these notions Grandma-and-Grandpa-to-be are quite careful not to examine them too closely. One suspects they guess how empty of thought the slogans really are. One guesses they are also not so happy when they show up in church on a certain Sunday after Easter and find those empty slogans threatened by—precisely—Acts 4, one of the featured lessons for the day. To be sure, that unhappiness is quickly soothed the moment they notice how the pastor hurries through his reading of it, especially at verse 12; and even more when they also notice him steering widely clear of it in his preaching.

Why he does so is obvious. Careful and attentive he is, well versed in the joys and griefs of his flock. He therefore knows only too well that Grandma-and-Grandpa-to-be's troubled intimations are shared all too widely within the congregation. What has happened, of course, is that the anxiety of the Constantinian missionary's child has come home to roost in post-Constantinian America. "What," said the child, "became of all my playmates' great-grandparents who happened to die before Dad showed up to preach the Gospel in this place? For that matter, what shall become of my playmates themselves and their good, kind parents who, polite though they be, have made it quite plain that the word of the Gospel is not for them?" There is, of course, nothing new about these questions, nor about the range of answers which the Church's wise ones have proffered for them.[11] What is new, and a direct consequence of the revolution, is that North American Christians should find themselves having to ask the questions no longer occasionally, about people they imagine, but now continually, about people they know, and often love. Gone for good is the old defense of the culture's expectation that everybody *ought* to go to church, read the Bible, and, yes, believe in Jesus, the effect of which was to discourage patent disbelief, or at least keep it from view, even as it allowed one more readily to accept the implication that weeping and gnashing of teeth were appropriate outcomes if not for Catholics, then certainly for scoffers.

But scoffers—Ted Turner comes to mind—and disbelievers-in-Christ are now the cultural norm, and often the role model. Why this is so is, I repeat, for others to account. That it is so is precisely why the faithful, and with them

their pastors, find themselves suddenly scrambling to keep
their balance in what they perceive as a clash of conflicting
demands, of basic civility, on the one hand, and of confessional authenticity, on the other. One of civility's demands
is that one should not place demands on the neighbor.
Another is that one should not merely think well of the
neighbor but should hope well for the neighbor also. Both
seem increasingly impossible to achieve in North America
by one who embraces the "no other name" confessional
vigor of St. Peter in the temple courtyard. The disbelieving
neighbors are these days simply too many. All too often
they're too near and dear.

More and more, North American Christians are resolv-
ing this struggle for balance by backing away from the force
of their Christian confession. The move is entirely under-
standable. It is easier to opt for the neighbor one sees than
for the apostle one does not see, especially an apostle so
ancient and hidebound, so intolerant, to use the epithet
du jour. Whether the choice between neighbor and apostle is in truth as real as it appears, we will examine later.
For now it suffices to note that the choice is being made,
and the apostle is losing, at least among Lutherans (thus
the import of the aforementioned survey). But if the apostle is losing among Lutherans, then he is surely also losing
among their mainline Protestant cousins, among segments
of the Roman Catholic faithful, and even, one reasonably
surmises, among portions of the evangelical flock, however firmly its officialdom may urge what it perceives to be
the apostle's cause. Evangelicals, too, are bound in turn of
the millennium North America to be yoked, many of
them, to the disbelieving son-in-law. They, too, rub shoulders daily, all of them, with the defiantly unchurched:
neighbors, coworkers, and in some cases even friends who
brandish their rejection of Christian claims as a Right,
"god-given" as they may even say. Or, catching themselves,
they will cite an authority they deem of equivalent majesty,

starting of course with the First Amendment to the U.S. Constitution.

Rubbing such shoulders and recognizing also the essential human decency of many to whom these shoulders belong, one's neighborly impulse is bound to kick in. When in the grip of this impulse one turns to a superficial consideration of the Gospel—the level, unfortunately, at which consideration too frequently stops—the Gospel is equally bound to sound less and less like the most excellent news the apostle asserts it to be. The problem, of course, is the apostle's presentation of the Gospel—his account of God's doing for the world in Christ Jesus, and with it his announcement of who, why, and to what end Christ presently *is*—as something to be believed. But this is the very thing that neither neighbor nor son-in-law is willing to do, finding it, as they may say, implausible at best, at worst outrageous and hegemonic. Against this stands the apostle's inescapable implication that those who refuse to believe the Gospel are ipso facto excluded from its benefits.

At this point the thoughts begin to crowd: can God indeed be so mean, so shabby, so *limited* as this? Can salvation's door in truth be that narrow? One hates to offend the neighbor, lovely person that she is, with the implication that she might be mistaken or wrong—or still worse, endangered—in her dismissal of Christ. One hates even more to think that the disbelieving son-in-law will land in hell. Hell, however, is exactly where St. Peter's fearsome words would seem to leave him, taking no account, as they do, of his track record as decent husband, doting father, and all around good Joe. For his sake, for the children's sake, one thrashes about for words other than these to hang one's hopes on.

More and more, pastors are finding themselves under pressure to supply these words. It rolls toward them from the pews on Sunday morning. At least for mainline types it throbs away in the background of a seminary training that

featured an extended swim in the tides of postmodern theory, exegetically and theologically applied. For one and all
it bubbles up from their own daily encounters as neighbors
and fellow citizens with the unchurched, their legions
lately augmented by a wave of non-European immigrants
whose religious commitments, frequently firm, are other
than Christian. The pressure's thrust is to "fix" the
Christian Gospel by drawing the fangs of its Christological
particularity. Let the preacher proclaim the reign of God or
the ministrations of the holy angels. Let her wax eloquent
of human possibility, let her dole out bromides for the
soothing of human pain. Let him by all means encourage
good works, and in doing so let him by no means hesitate
to hold up Jesus as encouragement and best example to us
all of this, that, or the other life-enhancing virtue. (All the
better if he does so wearing a WWJD bracelet as inspiration
to the kids.)[12]

What we the hearers will wish our preacher *not* to do,
however—so scream our first instincts—is to join the apostle in preaching of Christ *necessarily* incarnate and crucified "for us and for our salvation"; in whom alone resides
any conceivable human hope of standing at last and forever
in the merciful presence of God. Such a Gospel can be but
"gospel," good news only so-called, nested of post-
Constantinian necessity in the quotation marks of the
skeptic. For in a land and a culture such as ours now is, it
stinks too strongly of arrogance. Worse, it screams threat,
not promise, portending as it does the standing of too many
decent and deserving people—people *we* know—in the
teeth-gnashing bitterness of ultimate darkness.

And still worse, indeed worst of all: such a "gospel"
seems these days utterly indefensible. The preacher, ignoring our knee-jerk wishes, may dare to tell it. We its hearers,
steeped though we be in the platitudes of the regnant culture, may nonetheless dare in some measure to believe it
("for ourselves" we quickly add, obeying the platitudes).

What we surely cannot do, however, is claim to *know* it. Against neighbor and son-in-law we obviously cannot *prove* it. And when they tell us that ours is "but one religion among many"; when, shoving harder on the knife, they sneer that what we say of God-in-Christ is "merely our opinion"; and when, with a final twist of the wrist, they aver that God, if there be one, merciful and good, will surely save them, connection to Christ or lack thereof entirely notwithstanding: then we know not what to say; and we stand ashamed before them; and the ensuing silence is dreadful.

Therefore, dear preacher, and for all these reasons, speak more of God, speak less or not at all of Christ; and when the day's texts, doing as apostolic texts are bound to do, toss up this dreadful business of the *solus Christus,* fudge them. Critique them. Edit them. Better still, ignore them. Don't make us hear them. For our souls' comfort, dig up something else to preach about today.

On the Nature, Logic and Character of Apostolic Confession

1. Nature

Today's preachers, so pressured, do well to remember that none other than Peter, their famously intolerant predecessor, knew something of the same pressure. So did his colleague Paul. The former therefore reflects openly on the nature of the Gospel as the rock of stumbling (*petra skandalon,* 1 Pet 2:8). The latter sounds the same note, of course, with the further comment that "the word of the cross" is, if not "stumbling block," then certainly "folly," depending on the ear it happens to strike (1 Cor 1:23). That both should be driven to acknowledge this cannot be surprising. There is less that separates pre- and post-Constantinian sentiments of the divine than young post-modernists might care to think. Our ideas are not new. Nor is our sinner's God-defining hubris. Nor is our laudable concern for the eternal welfare of friends and dear ones who spurn Christ. Indeed, Paul himself shares that concern, as Romans 9–11 makes plain.

Both men, feeling the pressure, refuse nonetheless to mute the Gospel's scandal. Both continue unrelentingly to proclaim Christ Crucified as the be-all and end-all of salvation, the *sine qua non* of life with God. Thus Peter's Pentecost sermon, which, from the point of view of essential content, sets the standard of all Christian proclamation that follows, not least the proclamation one encounters in the more mature reflections of his own first letter. Thus also Paul, who both echoes and reinforces Peter's central point, that "God has made him both Lord and Christ, this Jesus whom you crucified" (Acts 2:36; RSV). In Paul's case one thinks especially of that wondrous lyric, Phil 2:5–11, to my mind the teleological nugget of the entire New Testament, by dint of its terseness more precious still than the gemlike opening paragraph of Revelation 21. "This," Paul avers, "is the point toward which humanity tends, the one at which all people must ultimately arrive, every knee bowing at Jesus' name and every tongue confessing that Jesus Christ is Lord to the glory of God the Father." He leaves unspoken the further reflection of Matthew 25, that some tongues will confess the Name with sheeply joy, others with goatish lamentation.

Quite inconceivable to Paul and frankly excluded by his proposal is the conceit, more common still to the first century than to our own emerging twenty-first, that come the eschaton some tongues might still be heard confessing Zeus as Lord, or Osiris, or, worse still, Moloch. Equally excluded is that other conceit, rife now if not then, of finding oneself in that day with mute tongue, no name at all being confessed, as in the 1998 movie *What Dreams May Come* featuring Robin Williams as the prototypical American suburbanite who cavorts hither and yon through a heaven from which God or any semblance thereof seems altogether absent. Such a concept, to Paul and Peter both, is bizarre beyond comment. That it soothes American souls—and this it does; witness the endless recurrence of the idea in the stuff of popular culture—would not persuade them to withhold from it their withering contempt. They might observe that a god-less heaven is a contradiction in terms. They might cite it as further evidence of the sinner's penchant, arrogant and misbegotten, to settle for vastly less than God in his mercy is determined to give. They would in any case dismiss it as blatantly untrue.

One senses, after all, that Peter and Paul not only believe that Jesus is Lord; they know it. Granted that the second letter in Peter's name is likely not from Peter's hand, even so the crucial assertion of 1:16 surely springs from Peter's mouth and mind, "For we did not follow cleverly devised myths when we made known to you the power and coming of our Lord Jesus Christ, but we were eyewitnesses of his majesty." Similarly with Paul, who engages the religious pluralists of the Areopagus (Acts 17) with a certainty that transcends believing, partaking vividly of the kind of knowing that the now sainted Lesslie Newbigin so ably describes for the illumining of the Areopagites' postmodern children.[13] Impudent it may be to deflate the pluralists' hope in their familiar deities. Scandalous it surely is to assert for all, American suburbanites included, an ultimate engagement with Christ, whether in saving embrace or in damning confrontation. Yet if it be true that Christ is Lord, and the apostles know it is, then the scandal must be borne, the impudence ventured. Copernicus is not about to keep his heliocentric convictions to himself on the paltry grounds that his contemporaries, committed geocentrists, will find them implausible, demeaning even, and are certain to take umbrage. For his part Copernicus not only believes better, he knows better. He therefore says so, and suffers the consequences.

Thus also the apostles, albeit fifteen centuries earlier, in their brand new knowing of the Christocentric universe.

2. Logic and Character

By virtue of their direct contact with the Lordly One who now sits at the heart of the universe, the apostles know this about him as well, that he is inexpressibly good. They therefore commend him to others with courage and joy. Their vigor of expression notwithstanding, one expects they do so also with humility. Each after all has been driven at a profoundly personal level to recognize how faith in this Jesus and the consequent knowing of his goodness is neither less nor other than a sheer gift which he himself bestows, if not directly then through the agency of his Spirit. Paul reflects this humility when he characterizes himself as "the least of the apostles" and the "one untimely born" who once, in disbelieving madness, had persecuted the Church. For his part, Peter carries the searing memory of a crowing cock; thereafter of a gentle voice unaccountably inviting him to "feed my sheep."

Suddenly we find ourselves at the edge of something very like a paradox. Might it be precisely from these depths of their prior humiliation that their present vigor of expression now proceeds? I would argue it is; so that what sounds like egregious arrogance—Peter's "no other name," Paul's "no other gospel" (Gal 1:9)—is in truth an effusion of honest and holy humility adorned with the blossoms of recognition and gratitude. Salvation, says Peter, cannot be less or other than the present munificence and the otherwise unthinkable hope bestowed on me by the Name above Names. Gospel, says Paul, cannot be less or other than the astoundingly good news I began to hear and grasp even as I was writhing the death throes of my former life in the dust of the Damascus Highway. God, say both, simply cannot be better, and therefore dare not be other, than we have found God to be in Christ: reconciling the world to himself, not

holding our crimes against us, transforming us from hell-
bent slaves into inheriting sons of a new creation, said sons
and daughters living for now in the breathtaking hope of
their own complete renewal, body and soul, and this to the
everlasting "praise of God's glory" (Eph 1:12, 14). Against
such an account of God and salvation all else pales into
poverty and destitution, not least the proffered alternatives
of their own first century. Hades is no Lamb adorned
heaven, not by the longest of shots. In the race with God-
in-Christ as One to be glorified and enjoyed forever, Zeus
fails to make it out of the starting blocks. The problem,
these apostles might say, with current American fancies of
the hereafter is that Americans, hoping small, are settling
for so desperately little: incorporeal extensions of earthly
existence in the company of "loved ones" whose souls'
essence remains fundamentally unchanged from the
essence of sinner (albeit nice sinner) of which all were originally composed. The contrast between this and an everlasting company of resurrected saints, robustly alive in
body and spirit, simply cannot be more startling, especially
when one adds the fantastic grace note of God himself wip-
ing tears from every eye (Rev 21:4, quoting Isa 25:8). A
choice between these two hopes is no choice at all. If the
one be proclaimed, the other dare not be peddled. One
notes with interest that the intellectual elite of our own day
have long since emulated their first century counterparts
in spurning the popular hope. As they rightly recognize,
only fools will pine for something so fraudulent, so dismally
low rent. But when, in so spurning, they choose with the
likes of Marcus Aurelius to settle stoically for no hope at all,
either for the individual or for society, this merely cinches
Peter's point: apart from the salvation associated specifically
with Christ (forgiveness of sins, resurrection of the body, life
everlasting) the very term "salvation" lacks meaningful content. Paul's point too is thereby underscored: if one sets aside
the good news of God's wonderfully free doing for us in

Christ and the ultimate promise thereof, one is left with no
news for anyone at all that is wholly good in any final sense.

In other words, there *is* no genuine gospel other than
Christ's. Neither *is* there any genuine salvation apart from
the one this gospel proffers. Again, it is not arrogance that
asserts this, but rather a humbled recognition, rigorous and
stripped of pretense, of how things frankly are in the world
we inhabit with such as ourselves who do the inhabiting,
each and all of us finding ourselves inescapably stuck, with
Adam, in the postlapsarian condition of being utterly
unable to look God in the eye, or even to want this. Why
else should God be banished from the Robin Williams
heaven? The incredible wonder, and therefore the good
news, is that for such people in such a world there should
be any hope of salvation at all.

Hope there is, the apostles proclaim. It bears a name,
and the Name is Jesus. The Gospel is that God raised from
the dead and thereafter placed in the seat of ultimate
authority this One whom we denied, persecuted, and,
indeed, crucified for his audacity in presuming to forgive
sins. Acting audaciously from that very seat of authority,
this One has seen fit—we know not why; by grace we are
saved—to forgive our sins. This same forgiveness, bearing as
it does the promise of an ultimate and everlasting reversal of
sin's consequence, he extends to all who will hear and trust
it. Therefore we tell of it. We know of no news so good, of no
salvation so free, complete, and available to all. Though truth
be told, we cannot even conceive of another salvation, for
the simple reason that the Author of this salvation is Lord,
and not another. Were he not, then the hope in him of which
we tell is an empty fiction, nothing more than the obnoxious
scandal and useless folly its detractors perceive it to be.
Then we are still dead in our sins. Then there is no salvation,
precisely as the savvy secularists assert.

"But, in fact, Christ has been raised, the first fruits of
those who have fallen asleep." So trumpets Paul, famously

(1 Cor 15:20). The brassy tone bespeaks defiance, which is something other than arrogance. At its core one catches the ring of wonderment and awe, much the same ring that characterizes encounters with the resurrected Jesus in the several Gospel reports, St. Luke's in particular (24:12, 22, 32, 41). As one might paraphrase, "Such things ought not to be, but they are. Jesus is—astoundingly—Lord." There comes a point, of course, at which defiance passes into courage and awe gives way to wild joy. In Paul's case one finds that point most notably in the letter to the Philippians, where, "for the surpassing worth of knowing Jesus Christ [his] Lord" and for the sake of being "found in him," he regards all else as "rubbish" and gladly suffers "the loss of all things" (3:8–9). Being added to Paul's loss column these days, especially in mainline Protestant circles, is his reputation as the apostles' apostle, the voice of voices, save Jesus' own, for Christians to hear and heed. Of the two main charges commonly leveled against him, misogyny is easily the lesser and sillier. Graver by far is the claim that he excessively restricts the accounts of both divine reality and human possibility through his single-minded focus on the person of Christ. One might well expect this accusation to grieve Paul, indeed to anger him. One cannot think, however, that it would cause him to "revise his opinion," "rethink his position," or in any other way break faith with the One on whom his entire being is now joyously staked. Not a beat will he skip in his resounding iteration, again brassily defiant, of the essential Christian confession: Jesus *is* Lord!

On the Link between Confession and Proclamation

Peter and Paul have hardly been alone in the strength, passion, and joy of their Christian confessing. Joining them over the centuries have been millions of others, the vast majority of whom are known these days only to God and to their fellow saints in light. Here and there a name stands out for having made the confession vividly, with a vigor and prominence very like that of these chief apostles. Athanasius springs to mind, and, on the Mediterranean's other edge, Augustine; also Francis, and Luther, and more recently Barth; also John Paul II, for that matter. But brief enumeration does gross injustice to many thousands of worthy others omitted from the list. These are men, sometimes women, who have led the Church to confess the Gospel in the teeth of the charges against it, often hard and compelling charges that continue century after century to surface from the broader cultural milieu like rocks from the soil of a New England corn patch.

No matter the age, the charges invariably call attention to the Gospel's unrelenting character as religious scandal and thinking person's folly. One wretched effect of this, again in every age, has been to soften the Gospel's hold on the hearts, minds, and loyalties of the baptized, these baptized being always and inescapably obliged to participate to some extent, whether more or less, in the cultural assumptions of their day. There is no avoiding this. It is the "law of things as they are," hinted at (if not precisely meant) by sixteenth century Lutheran confessors when they spoke of the baptized person as *simul iustus et peccator*, at once wholly just and wholly sinful. Not even the Amish can cease being American, however hard they try.

There is, then, nothing especially new about the dynamics at work when today's North American preachers mount their pulpits or, alternatively, stroll down the aisle for a sermon "from the midst." We read out the great Christological texts and sense that the natives are restless. Athanasius, hypothetically among us, would observe that we can't know what restlessness is really all about until we've tried reading those same texts to a fourth century congregation of crypto-Arians. Pastors died in those days for refusing to succumb to the pressure and mute the scandal, met and stumbled over at the time in its Nicene form as deity copersonified in Jesus. Vital it was, the bishop would add, that these pastors should have been willing to die, or be banished, or at the very least hounded from their pulpits, lest through their succumbing the Church had died and the Gospel itself had perished from the earth.[14]

To this day their proclaiming successors reap the harvest of their steadfastness, a point commonly missed by postmodern revisionists who find it suddenly chic to sympathize with Arius and to sneer loudly about the foolish fuss over a silly iota.[15] Yet that fuss bears fruit every time a North American pastor puts into wondrous play the Word that makes alive and brings into being things that are not. A colleague tells of an eighty-year-old woman, then confined to a nursing home bed and now at blessed rest, who tearfully, haltingly confessed the sexual offense she had committed as a seventeen-year-old girl and then carried as a stone in her conscience for the next sixty-three years. "It was a moment," said he, "heavy with awe, and astonishing. I pronounced the absolution and her eyes shone with joy as I have rarely seen. She knew relief, at last, and peace, genuine and final."

Shining eyes I have seen in the course of my own labors, most memorably in the face of another woman, not yet so old as the other though far dirtier, I should think; also barefoot, bent, and haggard; to those around her patently useless and therefore despised to a degree that none but childless widows of the rural third world are obliged to endure. Crone-ish, she was. Yet as she reached greedily for the communion cup I held out to her, I suddenly caught the glint in her eyes and saw before me no crone but a radiant sister-bride of Christ, breathtaking in the splendor of her worth-beyond-measure to God.

Was this simply the fleeting fancy of a fevered young missionary who happened that day to be especially hungry for a little occupational validation? Looking back, I think not. I call it rather the consequence of obedience on both

our parts, the woman's and mine, to the authorizing word
of the One whose blood was in that cup, whose Holy Spirit
not only drives us to hear the word and obey it (in this case
"the blood of Christ, shed *for you*") but also and graciously
affords the occasional glimpse of things to come on account
of that word. The point is that neither my colleague nor I
could have seen what we saw had it not been for pastoral
predecessors who refused so long ago to diminish the scandal of the absent iota, pressed though they were in the ever
cited interests of tolerance and good sense to do just that.

It does matter, immeasurably, that Christ is of one
being, not merely of like being, with the Father. Therefore,
his Word in the mouth of his authorized public representatives is indubitably and unshakably God's Word. Therefore,
stricken old women, addressed by these representatives in
Christ's name, have something firm, not spongy, to grab
hold of, allowing the one to rest in marvelous peace and the
other to head home after the service with new heft in her
hobble, both having tasted the joy beyond understanding
which Paul and Peter knew and which, in fruition, is precisely the emotive content of their salvation to be, assured
and everlasting. And other things, too: therefore parents
get to glow when their babies are baptized; therefore a wife,
forgiving her errant, repentant husband, can live on with
him in the certainty that the mantle of Christ's righteousness now covering his shame is no figment of her wishful
thinking but the very thing that God Himself beholds as He
looks on. Therefore, too, the groping, disbelieving world
can gasp as one Karla Faye Tucker, recently notorious as
the Texas pickax murderer who finally found Jesus (or
better, says the orthodox Lutheran, whom Jesus finally
found) lies down on her execution gurney without a fuss
and confidently accepts the lethal injection.

And therefore every pastor, going about her duties faithfully, will these days find herself at some point in the middle of the following scene. She stands with the family at a

hospital bedside even as the patient breathes his last. Spouse and children begin to sob. The doctor, chancing in, averts his eyes and slinks silently away, shoulders slumped in defeat. The other eyes in that room now swing to the pastor, who stands suddenly tall. As if in a flash of compelling insight she knows she is blessed with something to say that begs its own saying, so good it is, so useful and true and redolent of hope: one final word to be uttered by her on the authority of the Word who was himself dead and buried flesh precisely for the sake of this newly minted corpse, that it might live again, although not merely again, Lazarus-like, but wholly made new. "Death, where is thy sting?" the pastor intones. "Where, grave, thy victory?" Again Athanasius, hypothetically looking on: "What then are a few pastors' lives, still less my own long exile and brutal contention? For rewards like these, still ongoing, the price we paid sixteen hundred years ago was small indeed. Did we not do well to pay it? Are you not now deeply glad that we stayed the course, resisted the pressure, clung stubbornly to our narrow, focused convictions and preached the Gospel as it was, and is? Knowing that this Gospel always grates in proud and sinful ears, we refused to parse our telling around the troubled implications our hearers drew from it. Instead we let the scandal stand, the scandal of Jesus Christ, co-equal with the Father, God and Lord for us *and* for all. 'All' at the time included all of you. Will you dare to do as we did, that the Word, now working its wonder for you through us, might yet do the same for others through you?"

"So I pray," says the bishop. "Amen and Amen," shouts that host of his co-confessors from the Church's every age, the present writer frankly among them. Then comes another cry, again the great "Amen," this one louder by far, magnificently glad, but also somehow tinged with a note of special pleading. Somewhere buried in that second shout are the voices of some grieving children, a dead criminal, a wounded wife, a happy set of parents—and two old women.

Are today's pastors feeling this pressure?

Cultural Constraints and the Work of God

Oddly enough, those pastors who do feel this other pressure and are eager to respond to it can find some encouragement for doing so in the nature and character of the very culture that seems, at first blush, only to oppose them.

One of the characteristic features of postmodernity, say the specialists, is the freedom it affords the individual to select for himself a set of principles by which to shape his conduct, identify his goals, infuse his work with meaning, and ennoble his life with a sense of purpose. Classic Christian theology is appalled by this, of course, correctly reading it as sinner's hubris gone mad. Eating from the tree of the knowledge of good and evil has degenerated into swinish gorging, and the gluttons, no longer content merely with leaping into the seat of divine authority, are now dancing a jig on it.

Yet Luther, characteristically looking at such things from more than one angle, also joins Paul (Rom 1:24) in understanding the aggravation of sinner's arrogance as a consequence of divine action. This is God's "alien work," as Luther calls it, whereby the sinner is driven into such confusion and eventual despair that she will at last be receptive to God's "proper work," i.e., his action in Christ to rescue and save her. "Alien work" might these days be heard more intelligibly as "tough love," or, in Twelve Step movement terms, as "being forced to hit rock bottom."

Be this as it may, the notion that God might have a jabbing finger in the development of the postmodern sinner's mindset is intriguing, to say the least, particularly in light of a fascinating irony which attends that mindset. For even as it shrinks from assertions of universal truth, Christian or otherwise, it also leaves the door wide open to the act of making those assertions. Pastors do well not to miss this. It presents them with a distinctly useful advantage as they go about their essential task of proclamation, especially if and as they do so with due attention to what the Church has historically insisted on proclaiming. The advantage is this: under the terms of postmodernity, pastors are as free as anyone else to "construct their own reality." One might go so far as to say that pastors are expected to do this, especially by their hearers, but by onlookers as well. One can hardly quibble if the reality so constructed embraces others, as any one person's reality necessarily must unless that person be a Robinson Crusoe in his "pre–Man Friday" period. Standing in their pulpits, pastors therefore find themselves under a *cultural* obligation to propound a distinct and particular worldview that embraces the hearers without pandering to them, whether with undue reference to their fears and foreboding or, worse, through excessive attention to their whims and predilections. The latter especially is deemed a mark of fraudulence, in preacher and politician alike.

"Authenticity" is the key. Again fascinating is that this word, so central to the values of postmodernity, should spring from the same root and participate in the same family of meaning as "author" and "authority." One senses in these latter days a recurrence of that first century ache for those who teach "with authority, and not as the scribes" (Mark 1:22). Thus, for example, the phenomenon of a Dr. Laura Schlessinger, the radio psychologist whose snide, know-it-all contempt for her listeners and callers serves merely to multiply them. Granted that odium of her sort is not to come within ten miles of the pulpit, discomfiting sermons authentically urged will likely be better received by postmodern hearers than soothing, agreeable ones that reek of weakness and insincerity. At millennium's turn one of the largest, most vibrant churches in the Greater Cleveland area is presided over by a transplanted Scotsman whose Calvinist rigor would do John Knox proud. He "tells it like it is." He vividly believes what he tells. By all accounts, upper-crust suburbia can't get enough of him.

What that Scotsman is doing with the Law of God can surely be done also with the Gospel. Indeed it must be done. So much the better for suburbanites and all other cultural subspecies of contemporary North America if the message forthrightly told is less the obvious account of human transgression and God's abhorrence thereof, much more the strange apostolic account of God's incomprehensible folly in responding to that transgression as he has, and does, in Christ. If scandal should attend this telling, so be it. Our initial intimations of hearers' reactions too easily betray us. Closer examination reveals no reason inherent in postmodernity itself for covering the scandal up. Instead one discovers abundant reason for setting the Gospel forth, scandal and all, if only provisionally, as another statue in the Areopagus, another option for choice-drunk seekers to explore in their quest for self-definition.

But if the Gospel is to receive serious attention as an authentic option—and this it assuredly merits; even those who have rejected it will admit that much!—then those who set it forth are obliged to do so authentically, better still with the authority of blunt and patent confidence. The necessity of doing so is beyond argument. I will explore something as potentially good and true "for me" only when those who tell me of it manifestly believe it to be good and true at least "for them." But I will look at it even more closely when, after the fashion of apostles and confessors, they also radiate a conviction that what and Whom they speak of is good and true for all.

Of course if the Gospel so proclaimed is good and true, then the promise of a faith-inducing Holy Spirit which attends it will surely bear its fruit in hearts that are finding their rest and their hope in Christ. That such hearts may presently be found in abundance throughout North America is also beyond argument. Ask any pastor who has not balked at the Gospel's scandal, who has continued to proclaim it with a reasonable measure of apostolic fidelity, and who knows his flock, or hers. So it is, following Luther, that God's "proper work" is getting done, also under the conditions of postmodernity.

Pastoral Purpose Revisited

By the grace of this God who insists still on hurling the Word and Spirit of Christ into the world, our young graduate, now wearily driving his moving van down Main Street, Buzzard's Beak, has something of profound purpose and high eschatalogical moment to expect when once he finds the parsonage, unloads his belongings, endures that day or two of nervous preparation, and then at last steps up and forward to cut loose before the flock with his brand-new pastor's first sermon. If only he will believe this.

Beginning with that sermon and extending thereafter throughout his stay in this congregation, his fundamental job, task, and calling will be to join apostles and confessors of every age in proclaiming the Gospel as effectively and unrelentingly as he can. As he does this, his aim is to entice as many tongues as possible, whether in his own pocket of the globe or elsewhere, to start confessing with joy that Jesus is Lord in high and holy anticipation of the day to come when every tongue in heaven and on earth will be doing precisely the same (Phil 2:11).

This, after all, is what the Gospel is for, and the Church as well. It cannot be otherwise, not when the Gospel, by definition, is the good news of Jesus Christ the Son of God (Mark 1:1) and the Church, again by definition, is the union of people with Christ (Matt 18:20; 1 Cor 12:12; Eph 2:20).[16]

Proclaiming this Gospel is what pastors are all about—nothing more, and nothing less; or so suggests this Lutheran who thinks the forebears of his own tradition were on to something when, in the fifth article of the

Augsburg Confession, they said that the office of the ministry *is* the Gospel.[17] Strikingly absent from this definition
of ministry is any reference to persons, ordained or otherwise. The logic of this becomes transparent the moment
one realizes that the Augsburg confessors are describing
God's ministry to the world whereby dying sinners are
connected by faith to the Christ who authorizes their justification and makes them alive. The vehicle of this ministry,
and also its content, is therefore the Word of Christ that we
hear or sacramentally engage and are drawn to believe.
With respect at least to hearing, it matters not from whose
lips the Word tumbles, whether a pope's as he addresses
the crowd from his Vatican balcony or an illiterate third
world mother's as she teaches her toddler to pray. Both
pope and mother are ministers, agents of God's ministry,
i.e., the Gospel. Obviously there are vastly more of the latter than the former. Equally obvious is that where toddlers
are concerned the latter are vastly more effective, as ministers, than the former. The reason is simple. Toddlers trust
mothers. By popes they are merely bemused. Therefore the
role of pope, over against toddler, becomes at best a secondary one in which he uses the Gospel to encourage the
mother in her pressing call as front-line minister of the
moment.[18] As with pope, so also with any other pastor,
including our colleague at Buzzard's Beak.

Standing in his pulpit the new pastor surveys a gathering of God's ministers. Each has been authorized in Holy
Baptism to put the Gospel's vivifying word into play, even
as their pastor does. One does not have to be ordained,
after all, to extend the refreshing cup of forgiveness to one's
spouse or sibling in Jesus' name. Nor is a collared neck
required for speaking quietly with a neighbor about the hope
one harbors in Christ; indeed, in this case the lack of a collar
is more likely than not to lend one the ministerial advantage.
Collectively these ministers are a multifaceted manifestation
of Christ's presence in the world.[19] Individually they function

as the primary agents through whom the promise of new creation infiltrates the crevices of the old. At the heart of both infiltration and manifestation is a willingness on their part to embrace the Church's essential confession, living from day to day and week by week in the conviction, individual and collective, that Jesus is indeed Lord, and not another.

It falls to the minister in the pulpit to remind them of these things. Doing so entails his own incessant wording of the Gospel, primarily for their sake. His aim is the goal set forth by his apostolic predecessor in Eph 4:11–13, a mature identification on the part of "all God's people" with the ministry and service of Christ. His task is not an easy one. Chances are very good indeed that most of these ministers in the pews are not presently thinking of themselves in these terms. Nor will they be quickly happy to start doing so. Some, older ones especially, will be suffering the Constantinian hangover of understanding themselves almost exclusively as recipients of ministry. To lay claim to a ministerial identity as Gospel agents will therefore strike them as grossly presumptuous. Others, drenched from birth in post-Constantinian assumptions, will still be stumbling badly over the Gospel's character as particular truth for all, and will be unwilling to countenance a direct role in its propagation.

In light of this, the pastor immediately faces a two-fold challenge: first, to arrive at a fuller understanding of how it is that cultural assumptions of his flock are impeding their Gospel confession; and second, to ascertain a way of surmounting these impediments. It is to the first of these challenges that I now turn.

2

The Gospel as Proscribed Speech

What I have written so far rests on the following axiom: The Church, called into being by the Spirit of Christ, exists for the purpose of confessing that Jesus is Lord. It does so now in confident anticipation of that great day to come when every tongue will do the same, to the glory of God the Father (Phil 2:11). It does so in all its many facts and acts, whether of organizing, gathering, praying, proclaiming, serving, or challenging, insofar as these attest to the present and enduring authority of the One in whose Name these things are done. It does so because it has no other adequate reason for being. Why else shall the Church be called Christian?

This said and confessed: it is one thing for God's minister, the pastor, to make the Church's confession from her pulpit. Flinch though some might as she holds forth on both implication and ramification of the Lordship of Jesus, all sitting before her will agree with the sour old rams, previously cited, that this is what she's supposed to do and is paid for doing in this setting.

It is quite another thing for God's ministers, the baptized laity, to make this same confession as they go about the details of their daily lives, or even as they attend together to their common life and business as members of a Christian congregation. Confession is a form of highly intentional communication. At some point it necessarily involves speech, the employment of particular words about the particular thing being confessed. Pastors are specifically trained in the use of the Church's language. They are also typically expected to employ it, at least as they go about their official duties. All too often the laity do not receive such training. Worse, they live day by day with an expectation that even if so trained they will have the good sense and the civility to conceal the fact and keep their conversation confession-free. And so they do.

In this chapter, I intend to explore this phenomenon in two stages. The first, a case study, describes my encounter with the phenomenon at a congregation I served not so long ago. In the second stage I attempt to uncover the roots of the phenomenon through a cross-cultural analysis.

Driving the exploration are the following questions: why do large numbers of North American Christians typically shrink from articulating their faith? Why are the singularly good words, "Jesus is Lord," so much harder to say in North America than in certain other parts of the world? Again, why are the healing, transforming words Christ has authorized us to utter so infrequently used by North American churchgoers, and not only in their dealings with the stranger but also in their intramural conversation? And finally, what, if anything, can be done about this?

But this final question takes us beyond the bounds of the present chapter into the one that follows.

First things first. To illustrate the validity of the questions I have raised, I start with the tale of a church and a pastor I know.

Part I. Case Study

Notes on a Tongue-Tied Church

A fantasy: A groping, probing pastor, sitting around the table with members of his church council, begins pushing a series of eggheaded questions. "Why are we doing the things we're doing at this congregation? Why are we doing less of this and more of the other? On what grounds do we make decisions—unavoidably, there being countlessly more to do than we or any other group of Christians have the time, money, and energy for—about where to allocate, or concentrate, or direct our resources? What and whose purposes are we out to serve, and of these, which are paramount, and again, why?" To which one of those in attendance quietly responds, "Why, Pastor, what foolish questions you ask! Of course our purposes are those of the Lord Christ whose people we are; whose name we confess; whose paths we follow; to whose grace and cruciform glory we bear witness in word and deed, in countless ways both large and small. This said, let's get on with our discerning and deciding. A prayer for the Spirit's guidance might be in order."

Such was the stuff of my wistful dreams in the early 1990s, about the time I began to think in earnest about the matters at issue in this essay. Last chapter's fiction of Buzzard's Beak had recently become my reality, except that I found it unfolding not in Montana but on the other side of the continent, in New England, three or so years removed from an initial stint of pastoral and theological service in the Papua New Guinean stomping grounds of my childhood. I leave the town in New England unnamed, observing merely that it was one of many that was busily abandoning its roots in farming and light manufacturing for a new career as a commuters' exurb. The church I will call Trinity, a solid Lutheran alias.

I note for the record that I came in my years at Trinity to hold its 220 active members in abiding love and affection. They were and remain what St. Paul is pleased to call the saints in Christ Jesus (Phil 1:1). I owe them all an apology, herewith extended, for having taken as long as I did to embrace this fact—if one can, strictly speaking, call it a fact. Better, perhaps, to describe it as an obvious and happy implication of another fact, this one evident and demonstrable, that the Gospel, preached in their hearing, was being responded to, and this from the moment I took office as their fifth full-time pastor.

Unfortunately, such responses as were there to be seen I either did not see or else failed sufficiently to acknowledge during my first year or two among them. This was in part because I was too busy looking for other responses that were not there to be seen, in part also because I was preoccupied, especially in the beginning, with anxieties that lurked in the deeper recesses of my own navel. At their heart lay the struggle of a man in his mid-thirties to believe that the proposition "Christ is Lord" is worth spending one's life on, especially when that spending is done in the obscurity of a small church in a small town amid too many signs, suspiciously construed, that the people you're serving could get along just fine without you. Frantically occupied postmodern exurbanites are not typically prone to calling the church office during the course of the working day for a friendly chat with the pastor. The person who sits by that silent phone, therefore, needs quickly to learn the lesson urged by Stanley Hauerwas and William Willimon, that he or she is there for purposes other than "the meeting of people's needs"[20] Otherwise trouble comes, whether in the burnout Hauerwas and Willimon discuss or in bouts of grievous vocational doubt. I, for one, was too slow a learner. Be it said that the shabby salary, typical for churches of that size, did nothing to speed the learning and still less to ease the angst.

For their part, the faithful at Trinity were very glad I was there, as I eventually came to understand. In my initial conversation with the call committee (Lutheran for "search committee") I had been led to believe that the congregation, then verging on its centennial anniversary, was dispirited. On arriving I found it to be so. Anxieties were typical for an established congregation of this size, chiefly the unending question of how to pay the bills coupled with a sense (erroneous, as I discovered when I got around to the actual demographics) that the congregation was aging, with too few younger families available to assume the elders' burdens. Recent conflicts had aggravated the mood. Gripped in that mood, their sense of common purpose seemed to focus squarely on questions of organizational survival. My presence promised this survival; hence their gladness for it. In my own darker moods I was not so glad. Wanting the encouragement of a sufficient reason to be there, I looked and listened for someone other than myself to draw a connecting line between Trinity's purposes and the defining confessional purposes of the larger Church, in the name of which they had called me there. I looked and listened in vain.

Our moods brightened over the next couple of years as we came to know and like each other. That knowing and liking served in turn to ease the respective anxieties with which we'd begun. It helped when I unearthed from dusty seminary notes a functional definition of "church" which allowed me to conclude that Trinity was acting as proper churches do, manifesting activity in each of five key categories: worship, nurture, fellowship, outreach, and service. That this activity was often fitful, even surreptitious, mattered less than the fact that it was happening at all. I found this comforting. Meanwhile the flock was busy deciding that oblivion was not their fate. Again, small things helped: the bonhomie of regular postworship coffee hours, newly instituted; the fresh noise of a baby or two competing with the preacher; incremental improvements in attendance and giving. There came a point about four years into my stay with them when talk began to surface of initiating a building program. Many later insisted on giving me a lion's share of the credit for this marked swing in mood and direction, attributing it especially to my having preached and otherwise cared for them respectably well. In obedience to them I will fight my addiction to humble pie and accept this credit, though gingerly, provisionally, taking care to emphasize the *soli deo gloria* which I habitually keyed in at the end of my sermon manuscripts.

The common thread running through those manuscripts was an insistent naming of the Name and telling of the scandal: Christ Crucified in whom alone resides our hope of forgiveness, life and salvation, to use the shorthand of Luther's Small Catechism. I did not preach in shorthand. I took assiduous pains to use standard Christian vocabulary (sin, grace, faith) only sparingly, and then only with copious illustration. Theological jargon, including the Lutheran mantra, justification by faith, I shunned. Even so I preached the news that the jargon comprehends: Christ who makes us "all right" with God, which indeed we are when we trust this.

In short, I stood in their pulpit Sunday after Sunday proclaiming the Gospel as well and clearly as I could. I say this with as much objectivity as a person can muster in describing his or her own conduct. In so proclaiming I functioned as God's minister to them. I waited in turn for them to begin functioning openly as God's ministers to each other and thereafter to un-membered others. They did not; at least not openly.

Now is when the fantasy of the faithfully articulate church councilor began to haunt me. I had long been noticing that Trinity's members would rarely if ever discuss the reasons for their common congregational activity in ways that took account of its churchly character. To the extent that some such discussion and reasoning might be called for—in a casually reflective one-on-one conversation, let's say, or in an act of collective decision making—I would hear matters cast, almost without exception, in terms that were immediate, practical, and strictly secular. Thus "as a congregation we need to start encouraging more people to come to church." Why? Almost always, "Because right now

there are too few people carrying too great a burden in
meeting the budget"; never, "Because we are servants of
Christ with good news to tell." In circumstances where an
adequate naming of an activity's reasons would necessarily defy the limitations of nontranscendent language
("Why do *you* go to church so regularly?"), the reasoning
was certain to be truncated ("Because that's what we've
always done in our family"). More likely still, it was simply
dodged. I caught myself wishing this were not so. I won-
dered why it was.

At some point—pick the cliché—a penny dropped, a
light went on. Key to the aforementioned fantasy is an ability of the probing pastor's lay respondent to express herself
ably in explicitly Christian terms. Of course to talk this
way takes practice. I began to notice that I hardly ever
heard the vocabulary of faith being used anywhere at
Trinity by anyone besides myself except in the setting of
worship; and even there the words would be found in the
parishioners' mouths only to the extent that they were
directly prompted by the printed texts of the liturgy and
hymns. But once the service's final "Thanks be to God" had
been said and all had decamped downstairs for coffee and
conversation, then the "church talk" (God, Christ, Church,
sin, etc.) would be packed away for another week. If during
the week two members of Trinity should meet accidentally,
say in a supermarket aisle, their conversation would be
quite indistinguishable in terms of vocabulary and evident
thought pattern from that of your average well-mannered
pagan. Fair enough, one might think; the language of faith
is by no means required to buy groceries. Yet this conversational pattern persisted even when the meetings were
deliberate, taking place at church on church business.
Early on I had been struck by the oddity that such meetings would not begin with prayer unless I should be there
both to ask for it and then to lead it. One could hardly
help but wonder if there weren't a rule of sorts in place,

decreeing that words and expressions of faith were strictly off limits to unauthorized lay tongues.

Why should this be? At first I tried to chalk it up as the natural consequence of a self-perpetuating lack of practice, perhaps peculiar to congregation and place. That is, faith words were not being used at Trinity for much the same reason that a person, visiting in a foreign land, refrains from putting his sketchy knowledge of the local language to work lest he misspeak himself and feel foolish. Of course, in failing to speak he fails to learn and is consequently barred both from the language itself and from the thought patterns which proceed from it. Also with language the rule applies, "no pain, no gain," the validity of which one could surely see at Trinity. Perhaps I was also seeing an unspoken agreement among the linguistically unskilled to let each other's deficiencies stay hidden from view.

Yet there seemed to be more at work here than mere inability. Again I was struck by a dimension of the operative language rules that can only be described as territorial: church words in the church during church; in all other places at all other times, "normal words" only. A further analogy occurred to me: the immigrant's child who willingly indulges a parental penchant for the old mother tongue only within the four-walled sanctity of home sweet home, never ever out there among the English-speaking multitudes for fear of being revealed (and reviled) as one of "them foreigners." Even with siblings one adopts the unspoken rule of using English only. Inevitably one loses facility with the mother tongue, certainly for want of practice, but even more through a conscious act of will.

The analogy, I thought, was by no means extreme. On taking a moment to reflect on my own habits, I noticed how I had been observing territorial rules myself. As a pastor I was speaking in terms explicitly Christian only within distinct boundaries of time and place, wider and broader to be sure than those observed by the parishioners but nonetheless adhered to almost as strictly. Thus the contrast for example between my habitual confidence as official preacher and teacher on Trinity's turf and my flinching discomfort, deep and persistent, with the idea of evangelism, an activity which by definition required the transgression of spatial and verbal frontiers. Even when visiting lapsing parishioners I would find myself speaking to them in polite and careful terms about "returning to church." I would not, however, invite them forthrightly to the very thing that "church" is all about, namely a steady diet of the grace of God in their Lord Jesus Christ. But of course the dynamic at work with me in such an instance was not one of inability. It was surely not that I did not know what words to say. It was quite simply and bluntly that I would not want to say them, with the consequence that the churchly intention of that encounter, pastor with parishioner or whomever, would be obscured if not betrayed.

I noted two things. First, I had not been raised at Trinity. I could not therefore say that the inhibitions I was seeing in them were peculiar to them. Be it added that I'd encountered the same inhibitions in every other group of American Lutherans with whom I'd spent any time at all during the years of my adulthood.

Second, as with me, so with Trinity's congregants. They, too, were failing to give conversational evidence of their churchly character and purposes not merely because they could not, but especially because they would not. Their expressive barriers were in place not so much *de facto* as *de iure*. Looking again within myself, I saw a persistent inclination to account for this phenomenon as a struggle of faith and, more sharply, as a disinclination to embrace and proclaim the Gospel's scandal. No doubt it was this, to some large extent.

But I also recalled my prior years of pastoral service in Papua New Guinea, when I had operated with verbal rules quite different from those I was presently struggling under.

So had the ordinary members of the Christian congregations I encountered there. The contrast grated. It also accused. Above all, it begged for understanding.

Assessment

Trinity is but one of countless North American churches that might well be described these days as "confessionally challenged." So, too, its former pastor. A number of matters embedded in my description of our time together therefore require underlining.

First, there is something contradictory and somehow silly about a pastor who shrinks from pastoral words, indeed from the very words his vocation consists of, those wondrous ones of the Word made flesh around and toward whom his life's purpose is presumably ordered. Moreover, in the specific instance of the tentative conversation with a lapsed parishioner, one is struck by the inherently self-defeating character of an invitation that fails to spell out its essential content. Nor can one miss the foolishness of this failure when the invitation's neglected content is purported, by definition, to be the ultimate Good News.

Second, there is likewise something contradictory, self-defeating, and finally embarrassing about a congregation that appears to shrink from owning up to its Christian character for all but one of the 168 hours that constitute a week.

Third, I tell of these contradictions and embarrassments only because they are *not* our own; else I would have the decency to keep them to myself. For I have spoken of our shame. It is a shame widely shared, and not to be covered by the fig leaves of denial or self-justifying bluster. Over us all impends our Lord's grim expectation of a day when the Son of Man will find himself ashamed of purported disciples who spent their lives ashamed of him (Mark 8:38).

Fourth, a strictly functional definition of "church" in terms of characteristic activity—worship, nurture, fellowship, outreach, service—is finally inadequate as a description of what constitutes the Church in its local manifestations. Consider the following: Rotarians raise money by the heaps and do good deeds with it, even as nonprofits of all type and manner erect buildings for themselves and strive ceaselessly to expand their membership lists. For fellowship one can join a garden club or belly up to the bar with the Sons of Italy. Community colleges will gladly nurture the mind and morals, if not the soul of the average American adult, and Mormons pray. In other words, our land is awash in organizations doing the very things that churches do, and in many cases doing them better, with this sole and utterly distinctive exception, that only churches do them in the Name of Him by whom the Church is named, for Whom the Church exists, to Whom the Church bears witness.

Fifth, in the failure of churches like Trinity to name the Name and thereby clarify their identity there is surely some shrinking from the Gospel's scandal, in particular from the perception that outsiders will take umbrage at its hegemonic overtones as a word "for all." But there must be something else that lurks behind this as well. Otherwise one might reasonably expect silence toward outsiders while still encountering confessional volubility on the inside among kindred spirits and fellow believers. The latter is precisely what one does not find in churches of this ilk. It therefore serves as the springboard for further investigation along the following lines: whence these linguistic usage rules, so fiercely in force at Trinity, that keep members from expressing their common faith to each other? This is an urgent question. Adherence to the rules inhibits members from exercising a primary form of their calling as God's ministers. It bars them from the "mutual conversation and consolation of brethren" that Luther identifies as a fifth means of grace.[21]

Sixth, in churches where the Name is not named, one should reasonably expect to find an air of sadness arising from the pained wondering of members who sense intuitively the contradiction of a church that isn't Church and are being stung by its consequences. Purposes other than Christ's will be pursued and contested. Sufficient grounds for discriminating one goal from the next will not be available. One will hear from members their own wistful why: "Why is it that our congregation doesn't feel the way a church is supposed to feel?" There was much of this at Trinity, especially when I first arrived.

Seventh, as I also discovered at Trinity, the antidote to such sadness is the Gospel itself. I mention this only in passing, and anticipating the next chapter.

Part II. Analysis

Christian Utterance in Cultural Contrast

To restate my axiom: the Church achieves its purposes when, with confidence and joy, it bears witness to the Lord Jesus Christ, crucified and resurrected, ascended and awaited. Experience has taught me that it is much easier to bear this witness in other parts of the world. The contrast with the situation in North America is deeply instructive.

Consider the following episode, one that ran through my mind repeatedly during my early years at Trinity. The year is 1982. My family and I are living in a remote valley deep in Papua New Guinea's mountainous interior. Early one morning I hear a frantic rap on the door. The good friend and able Lutheran bishop whom I serve as an advisor has come with breaking news. It seems our neighbors are suddenly mustering in knee-jerk cultural reflex to do battle with members of an offending clan on the ridge above. Together we stride the two hundred yards or so from my back door to a spot on the main road where men have gathered in tense and loud commotion. Most are waving bows, already strung. Some are clutching spears as well. No one questions our approach. Our intention to say something, to bellow a protest against the surging emotional tide, is recognized and honored.

We speak. Our words, blunt, direct and, in that moment, profoundly countercultural, are those of the Lord and faith we represent. "Thou shalt not kill. Haven't you heard that somewhere before, gentlemen? What about that baptism you were baptized with, friend Poko? Weren't Malipu and the rest of the gang up there on the hill baptized into the same death and resurrection of the same Lord Christ? Is it not the same body and the same blood that you receive in Holy Communion? Haven't you been trained by birth and upbringing to prevent the shedding of your brother's blood at all costs? Must we assume that you're still buying in to the old falsehood that blood brotherhood stops at clan lines? How else can it be that you'd think to proceed, so wrongly and horribly, to spill the blood you share with your brothers in Christ up there?" And so on. We say this, mind you, without protest or challenge from our hearers; without so much as a hint of scornful, dismissive impatience. Nor do we see so much as a single eye gaze over with bemused incomprehension.

But what sticks most vividly in my memory is that all this is said in the open air of a public place, at a profoundly secular moment as we North Americans define such things, and yet the words feel entirely fitting and appropriate to both setting and moment, nor do I have any sense whatsoever of being out of place as I utter them. Not that the words are heeded, mind you. The pause to listen is only momentary, and then the battle begins. But whether the words are heeded or no is quite beside the point. Of the essence, so far as present purposes are concerned, is whether and where the words are spoken.

Thus I try to imagine myself speaking similarly to a pack of brawling youths on the streets of an American city—Cleveland, let us say—or to the shouting, red-faced adults at a nasty meeting of the local board of education. I cannot. For me, as for most people, willingness to speak is typically predicated on the minimal expectation, not that I will be heeded, but that I will be heard. Like most people I loathe rejection. Even worse is rejection larded with contempt. Yet such, surely, is the consequence for that person who, in these United States of the turning millenium, will attempt to exhort a group of publicly gathered strangers, using specifically Christian terms and concepts. One might as well demand that deaf ears be turned or that eyes should glaze. Were one to press the case, and somehow be spared the hoot or two of angry derision—how likely would that be in these days of widespread suspicion and downright hostility with regard to the so-called religious right?—one would surely not escape the sting of those patronizing, dismissive murmurs with which the polite slide past the rantings of the local mentally disturbed bag lady. At least, that's what the tensing muscles of my gut tell me as I think on such a scene.

Those gut muscles, both remembered and presently known, bear witness to a startling contrast between rural Papua New Guinea and suburban America. For a confessing Christian who wishes to speak her mind—to draw openly a serious, thoughtful, and realistic connection between the claims of her faith and the immediate realities of life, common and public—the former is a land of freedom and opportunity. The latter, for all its proud, noisy clamor about first amendment rights, is certain to strike her as a place of heavy repression.

I recognize that this is a sweeping assertion. Even so, I must decline to defend it, noting only that my gut is hardly alone in the witness it bears to the contemporary American situation.[22] Nor am I able, in this space, to trace precisely how this fundamentally cultural repression of the religiously devout, this discouragement and sanctioning of explicitly religious speech in public places, plays itself out in the practicalities of North American life.[23] I only note that all Christian confessors, no matter what their orientation in matters social and political, are subjected to it so that whether one is a Southern Baptist picketing the local abortion clinic or a member of the United Church of Christ waving an angry placard over the launching of the latest nuclear submarine, one is obliged to contend with the same cultural demand. Express your views—this is surely your right—but please and by all means keep your mouth shut about the One in whose name and for whose sake those views (presumably) are held. Of Him we will not hear. Of Him you may not speak.

I note also that the demand, more often implicit than explicit, for confessional silence frequently extends beyond the overtly public realm into activities commonly if not rightly understood as private.[24] For example, a faithful and conscientious member of a Lutheran congregation will feel free to invite a neighbor to come to church; she will not, however, feel free to invite that neighbor to come to Christ.

The question is why. This is the conundrum I wish to comprehend.

The Roots of Repression

In approaching this question, I find it helpful to return to the contrast between Papua New Guinea and North America as cultural venues for publicly asserting the claims of Christian faith. Again, the one seems to welcome and even encourage a free and open naming of the Name with all that the Name implies. The other brings powerful sanctions to bear against it. Why?

Reflecting on this, one is first and quickly persuaded of the foolishness of an explanation commonly advanced for the situation in North America, and more specifically in the United States. It is said, usually in the context of an attempt to account for an America remembered and the America presently known, that: (1) Americans today are suddenly confronted with a new pluralism of culture and religion. (2) This pluralism and the effort to comprehend it

are themselves responsible for an erosion of Christian confidence in general and for a growing ambivalence, at least
in the so-called mainline churches, about the validity of the
Church's evangelistic vocation, classically understood. (3)
The strengthening of social and legal sanctions against
explicitly Christian speech derives chiefly from the pluralistic imperative that all religious speech should be honored, valued, and protected. (4) This pluralism is in fact the
primary challenge with which the Church must come to
terms as it wrestles anew with the question of its mission
and purpose, especially in North America but also, by
extension, elsewhere in the world.[25]

As far as my present argument is concerned, the salient
feature in this line of reasoning is that pluralism per se is
somehow responsible for inhibiting specifically Christian
speech in other than private venues. But this is surely not
so. Papua New Guinea, where religious speech flies freely, is
the land of over seven hundred distinct and mutually unintel-
ligible languages. From an ethnolinguistic point of view, it is
the most diverse country on the surface of the globe.[26]

Whatever it is, then, that either gives free rein or applies
the bit to religious speaking, it is surely something other
and more than a mere plurality of culture and religion.
Speaking again and for the moment exclusively from personal experience, let me suggest what this something more
and other is.

Underlying the abundant pluriformity of Papua New
Guinean language, culture, and religion is a more or less
common telling of the basic structures of reality; a so-
called worldview, one that is vastly closer than the contemporary North American to the worldview assumed in
the Old and New Testaments.[27] Central to this worldview
is an assumption, so solid as to be beyond question let
alone argument, that reality comprises a dimension
beyond sensory perception, and even beyond perception
when perception is enhanced through instrumentation, or

by mathematical modeling. There *is* something there—classically the ghosts of the newly deceased; the forest spirits; the distant ancestors from whom "cargo" comes; the secret forces of nature, whatever these may be, that are nonetheless susceptible to manipulation through magic—something is there, inherently, which has a direct and immediate bearing on the shape and content of human lives. Any person of any sense or wisdom whatsoever will constantly pay it heed. Call it the spiritual dimension of life, the realm of the numinous, perhaps. It is so intertwined with the details of daily living, so deeply involved in the ordinary stuff of the world that its presence and influence must be taken into daily account with as much thoughtful seriousness as one accords the tending of a grove of coconut trees, or the building of a house, or the mending of relations with a neighboring clan. Things beyond our human control do not "just happen." In truth they are caused—intelligently done by an intelligence not our own.[28]

By definition, religious speech is concerned with the underlying, unseen structures of reality. Its purpose is to describe, discuss, and, if possible, comprehend life's spiritual dimension. In Papua New Guinea, religious speech is therefore as vitally useful, socially important, and indeed, publicly necessary as any other form of speech. Even more so, perhaps. In such a context when a missionary and a bishop begin speaking of the Lord Christ and his claims on the day's activities, people will listen on the utterly reasonable chance, as they see it, that these two characters might be rightly describing those numinous facts of life that everybody knows are there and must be attended to.[29]

By contrast, in North America people are simply not so sure about that numinous stuff.

So saying, I pause to note that the phrasing of this last sentence is quite deliberate. It is terribly important at this point to be careful in thinking and nuanced in writing.

For example, let's say that the local pastor, smitten by a spasm of foolhardiness, decides that he will in fact impart the counsels of divine Law (if not the sweet comfort of the holy Gospel) to a meeting of the typical New England Smallville's Board of Education. In contemplating the likely reaction to his speaking, his dismay can only be exacerbated by an all but certain knowledge that he will not have been addressing a religiously plural gathering. He knows going in, that is, that he is most unlikely to encounter any Hindus in that audience—or Muslims, or Buddhists, or Native American religionists for that matter. Here and there a Jew, perhaps. But indeed (this being Smallville and not West Hartford or Brookline, Mass.), chances are extremely good that every member of the Board and all but two or three of the concerned citizens present will, if privately pressed, identify themselves as Christian—as does, all the noise to the contrary notwithstanding, a suprisingly high 86 percent of all Americans.[30] To be sure, those Board members and concerned citizens are quite likely to think of themselves as religiously diverse, given that sloppy usage of the word "religion," still so prevalent in popular American speech, by which intra- as well extra-Christian distinctions are drawn, as in "What religion are you? Protestant or Catholic? Lutheran or Baptist?" But this in itself would hardly be an obstacle to a canny pastor intent on a genuine hearing. Mere misperceptions, even of long standing, can always be overcome.

Mere misperceptions, however, are the least of Pastor Foolhardy's problems. For he will encounter in that room a North American worldview, counterpart to the Papua New Guinean; a socially constructed and well-nigh unanimous consensus about the fundamental structures of reality. The piece of that consensus most wretchedly relevant to his intentions is a broad and deeply ingrained streak of what, for want of a better term, I will call a "spiritual agnosticism." Again, I choose my words most carefully. Thus, for example, the people in that room are almost certainly not religious agnostics. Many if not most of them belong to one of the local churches. Quite likely a majority of these are decently regular in attending mass or divine service, while the others will happily put in their Christmas, Easter, and rites of passage appearances.

By the same token, of the few present who are religiously disconnected, it is almost certain that none could be described as committed atheists, or as rank, dyed-in-the-wool materialists. These are, after all, Americans, inescapably immersed in a popular culture which, heedless of the intellectual grumps among us, continues as it always has to bubble and overflow with fascination for that numinous, spiritual dimension of life: Elvis sightings, the daily horoscope, psychic hotlines, the latest near-death experience, angels in the mid-90s, and the wizardry of Harry Potter at decade's end. Consider also the endless stuff of the visual media: the spirit seeking redemption in *Ghost*, the Force of the Star Wars series, the several talismans of Indiana Jones, the god-like if loathsome Q from *Star Trek: The Next Generation,* and on the darker side, Michael Jackson's *Thriller*, the umpteenth remaking of *Dracula*, and certainly *The X Files* with its ominous powers and principalities and its recurrent overlay of twisted Christian symbol. Such and more glue the masses to their screens. Meanwhile the more sober flock to lectures by the metaphysical guru of the day; or they keep the publishers of Carl Jung in business; or they save the spotted owl.

All of this suggests that North Americans remain vitally alive at least to the *possibility* (if not probability) that reality includes a something-beyond-perception. Like Papua New Guineans they sense that this transcendent, spiritual dimension bears somehow on the shape, direction, and eventual outcome of human lives.[31] Yet, while Papua New Guineans, as a rule, are highly confident that the spiritual dimension can be named, reasonably discussed, communicated with,

in some measure manipulated, and to a useful degree com-
prehended, Americans are deeply dubious about all these
things. The contrast here is one of epistemological stance,
between optimism, on the one hand, and pessimism, on
the other. Americans are the epistemological pessimists.
With respect to the spiritual we can wish, we can guess, we
can surmise, we can hope, we can certainly speculate, we
can even pray; the one thing we cannot do, most assuredly
(we think), is know. But if we cannot know—if the best
we can say about that unseen dimension is "I feel," "I
think," or "I believe" (note the singular tense of the
verbs)—then it does not matter how deeply we may be
convinced of its presence and influence. Nor does it matter
how committed we are to a specific description of it. We
can never be in a position to ask somebody else to order or
alter his behavior on the basis of what we have to say about
it.[32] Of course, neither is that somebody in a position of sufficient knowing to ask the same of us. For him to pretend
and attempt otherwise would be nothing less than an exercise in bald-faced effrontery.

Thus my term "spiritual agnosticism."[33] The fundamental truth claim of our culture with respect to matters spiritual is that we cannot know about them with anything
approaching sufficient certainty to command the allegiance
or shape the conduct or, least of all, correct the spiritual
and/or moral opinions of another. This truth claim, I suggest, is shared almost as widely and deeply by the churched
as by the unchurched, as I will shortly attempt to demon-
strate. In so sharing it helps to have discovered as a society
that however haunted we may be as individuals by our premonitions of the numinous we can nonetheless lurch along
from day to day and year to year, more or less effectively, it
seems, without enduring the social aggravation of having to
pay them collective heed.[34] Of course as any number of contemporary Cassandras and Jeremiahs would suggest, it may
well be that we simply have yet to comprehend the long-term

consequences of not doing so. Speaking of premonitions, they would argue there are surely signs aplenty in the land that the bill for this failure is coming due.

But then such voices, always strident, are for that reason alone too easily dismissed. For now the reigning consensus is that spiritual arbiters are neither needed nor wanted in public places, and if and when they appear on their own they certainly should not be trusted. Thus the fate which awaits our Pastor Foolhardy; who, by the way, might just as well have left his clerical collar at home. After all, this age is the so-called postmodern. Authority of all type and manner, but especially his, has been deconstructed. To one and all it seems perfectly obvious that if and as that spiritual "stuff" actually applies to the public matters at hand, then any one person in the room is as likely as he is to get it right, speaking as he so obviously is from his specifically white, male, heterosexual perspective. "Please, Madam Chairperson, spare us his pretensions."[35]

The Agnostic Assumption

Our sainted forebears of ages past, fond as they were of spiky polemic, would not have hesitated to call it the beast (Rev 13:5–8). I mean this streak of spiritual agnosticism, so deeply ingrained in the soul of contemporary North American culture. Its beastly effect on the apostolic purposes of the Church, the matter at issue in this study, is twofold. Externally, it hinders and suppresses an open, public confession that Jesus Christ is Lord. Internally, it saps the confidence of those who, through baptism, have been called upon to make that confession. In both venues, world and church, it proscribes Christian speech.

Hence, I submit, the problem at Trinity and churches like Trinity.

Luther, explaining the intent of the eighth commandment in his Small Catechism, enjoins us when speaking of the neighbor to "explain his actions in the kindest way."

This is a piece of common, everyday piety that runs deeply in me. I picked it up as a child through that osmotic process by which sons are shaped in the values of their fathers, and I cannot shake it. Only with the greatest care, then, do I suggest that one could detect a strong odor of the beast's presence in those rules and patterns of speech that lay at the heart of Trinity's problem. I mean, yet again, that pervasive refusal by Trinity's members to use the language of faith between themselves in settings other than formal worship, including the processes of organized meeting and casual conversation so necessary to the identification of essential purpose and the sifting through of common goals. The inescapable consequence of this refusal was that the congregation's churchly character and purpose could not be brought into open expression. Nor could members act as ministers of the Gospel, one to the other, thus gaining encouragement and confidence in their own struggles to believe and simultaneously developing their facility with the language so necessary to the fulfillment of their confessional calling.

I submit simply that the avoidance of churchly words at Trinity and churches like Trinity is best explained as a manifestation of North American spiritual agnosticism. How could it be otherwise? Swimming in that North American culture as fish swim in the sea, it should be no more possible for the members of Trinity to avoid having their souls permeated by its implicit assumptions than it is for the flesh of tuna to be free of the hint of salt. Or if by remote chance, better, if by the miracle of the Holy Spirit's grace, one or the other should find herself attuned, counter-culturally, to the epistemological confidence of the apostles, nonetheless she is obliged to expect that this same confidence will not be shared by those around her. Thus whether from within or without, or from both directions at the same time, all are necessarily beset by the agnostic assumption, that driving impulse to believe that

no single way of describing reality's unseen dimension can
be trusted. This implies, as an ethical corollary, that to
speak with confidence either of or from my apprehension
of this dimension is to risk infringing on your right to
apprehend and describe it as you see fit.

One is deeply trained in our culture to refrain from
"imposing one's religious beliefs on others." This is a common expression; in fact, so common that I can scarcely
imagine a member of Trinity who would not have been able
to rattle it off with the same unthinking facility and word-
for-word accuracy that in Cotton Mather's New England
was reserved for such things as the text of the Decalogue.
More than a few did precisely that while conversing with
me. Indeed, so deeply did the thought of this expression
run at Trinity, so embedded was the cultural imperative it
captures, that I would occasionally hear parents wonder
seriously whether they had a "right" to "impose their
beliefs" on their own children. No wonder, then, that avoiding God talk was regarded as the essence of basic civility in
the workplace or in the neighborhood, as any number of
Trinity's members vigorously confirmed for me, especially
when we got around to talking about evangelism.[36]

But if all this was so "out there," then it certainly made
sense also "in here," at Trinity, to avoid engaging in that
"mutual conversation and consolation" by which alone one
could gain practice and confidence in the words of faith
and the realities to which they point. Even with fellow
parishioners one ran the risk of giving deep offense by
claiming (or appearing to claim) priority for one's own
telling of the Unknowable. By far the safer and more civil
course was to keep one's "religious opinions" to oneself,
except that they be tentatively broached and ever so carefully couched in the verbal signals of uncertainty and open
question. Confident assertion, however, was a no-no. It
smacked of presumptive hubris. It implied transgression of

another's so-called space. For many it no doubt echoed with the harsh overtones of the culturally despised religious right.

Conclusion

Churches like Trinity are rightly understood as congregations afflicted by the agnostic assumption. Their members are crippled by the pessimistic epistemology of their natal culture. This renders it horrendously difficult, if not impossible, for the congregation to reflect and practice its identity as Church and, in so practicing, to act openly in accordance with its churchly vocation. The words on which that vocation depends are "off limits." Weirdly, Christians themselves become the enforcers of rules which work against the very Word in whom their life and purpose is found.

This raises the next question. How shall their pastors proceed in leading them beyond this impasse?

3

The Gospel as Required Speech

The Church's central and compelling purpose is to confess that Jesus is Lord. Yet churches shrink from the words the confession requires.

Church members are called to share in God's ministry of the Gospel. Yet these members are deeply unwilling to utter the words this ministry consists of.

Summoned to faith, North American churchgoers wallow in doubt, their hearts enthralled not by *Heiliger Geist*, the strong and Holy Spirit of our Lord and of his resurrection, but by *Zeitgeist*, the craven spirit of a bizarre age that believes in doubt. Tongues which the former would liberate are instead tied by the latter. Christ is not confessed, nor is the Gospel's ministry done. So it appears in all too many congregations. Of course I should really be saying "we wallow," not "they wallow." Pastors, too, are both perpetrators and victims of the agnostic assumption.

Hence the question which occupies this chapter: what and where is the way by which North American churches-so-called might become North American outcroppings of the Church-in-truth?

I submit from the outset that the key to this question lies in the Church's font and origin, namely the Gospel itself. This ought to be an unexceptional insight, though I suspect it is not, having taken too long to stumble over it myself. By Gospel I mean neither more nor less than the word of God's gracious and salvific doing in Jesus Christ on the world's behalf. By Christ's own testimony this word is intended for those who find themselves bound and beset (Luke 4:16–21). This surely includes people who are tangled in chains of erroneous cultural assumption. Among the afflictions from which the Gospel promises release are those which stem in significant measure from a failed or a deficient epistemology (John 8:31–36).

I intend in the pages that follow to explore how this might be so with respect to churches whose shackles, broadly cultural and sharply epistemological, are of the peculiar turn of the millennium North American variety. The path I explore is very much my own, although in treading it I am in conversation with any number of observers and theologians who have been writing and reflecting of late on the same themes I address. I seek a conceptual framework that will enable pastors to function with integrity as God's ministers to the tongue-tied agnostics who face them from the pews, to the end that these in turn will start to function with like integrity as God's ministers to each other, at the same time embracing their common confessional purposes as Church.

I speak of integrity. Integrity presupposes an honest and realistic telling of the truth of who one is. As Lutherans in particular are predisposed from the outset to anticipate, the matter of who one is, especially according to the Gospel, involves seeing a coin's two sides simultaneously. I offer this thought as an early indicator of the direction in which I am headed.

On Playing by the Rules

The quest for integrity leads me to begin in the rather odd place of asserting not only the possibility but the present danger within North American churches of heresy.[37] By heresy I mean claims, assertions, and proposals about the Church's faith and teaching which have the effect of subverting, contradicting, and ultimately supplanting the Church's confession that Jesus is Lord, capital "L." Heresy's inescapable consequence is that the Church winds up either dithering over its duties or else baldly pursuing purposes which are skewed, silly, and wrong.[38] There is altogether too much of this taking place of late in my own Evangelical Lutheran Church in America, not only on its theological fringes, but also in the culturally seduced hearts and minds of the otherwise faithful who comprise that church body's congregations.[39] I read of pastors waxing enthusiastic over a conference that pours contempt on the crucifixion and revels in neo-pagan invocations.[40] Meanwhile I listen as lifelong Lutheran parishioners speak with passionate conviction about reincarnation, and I watch as they circulate a popular book about a soul's trip to heaven and back in connection with a near-death experience, the climax of which is a supposed conversation with Jesus who calmly advises that all religions are of equal merit and validity.

Again we see the shades of that spiritual agnosticism which is open to everything and cheerfully confident about nothing. So deeply besetting are these shades that people seem entirely to miss the flagrant illogic by which Jesus himself is called upon to validate the popular conception of religion as a private, relativistic affair of the freely choosing heart. They fail to see how this radically undercuts the essential character of his own Gospel as genuine news both good and true for all people.

I suppose, of course, that Schleiermacher has something to do with all this for having made respectable the pietist's deadly shift in attention away from the externals of the Word to the internals of the consciousness. The history of American religious culture has much to do with it as well, reflecting already from the Puritan era an elevation and celebration of the individual's private experience over the public content of community traditions.[41]

At the same time American culture is rife with fascination over sports. Americans, therefore, certainly understand that to play any game one has to stick by the rules. Baseball stops being baseball the moment one asks the pitcher to lob basketballs across home plate. This point is strongly germane to the matters at hand. For as George A. Lindbeck has persuasively pointed out, religion is at least that: if not a playing, then a believing by the rules—or to put it more sharply, a speaking and doing by the rules.[42] If one wishes on philosophical grounds to dispute the claim that religion can describe objective reality (Lindbeck calls this claim a propositional or cognitive view of religion), still one must at least recognize that religion, like a given culture or language, is a comprehensive *interpretive scheme* of reality with a necessarily coherent system of symbols, formed and arranged by tradition, by which one organizes all of life in accordance with whatever it is that one takes to be "maximally important."[43] But to say this is also to recognize boundaries beyond which one moves into incoherence, or if not that, then into another and different interpretive scheme, much as, by uttering certain sounds, one moves beyond the pale of the English language and is found instead to be speaking gibberish, or perhaps German.

There is a point, then, at which one ceases religiously to be Christian. This can be said with anguish and anger as it usually will be if one takes a propositional view of things, or it can be said dispassionately as Lindbeck helps us to do.[44] But whether with fire or ice it ought to be said. Enough of dishonesty. To borrow that lovely triumvirate of terms from the Formula of Concord, if you wish to believe, teach, and confess other than as a Christian then say so, get on with it, and kindly quit claiming to be something you no longer are to the discombobulation of those you've left behind.

Assume instead that both they and you have more worth-
while things to do than to stand around arguing. As the
umpire says, "Play ball!"

On Tradition and Concession

Second point: I do not and cannot decide for myself what
it means to be Christian. I learn it. I discover it from others.[45] I can accept it or reject it to be sure, but if the latter
then I forfeit my right to claim the name.

Once learned and discovered, of course, I put the content of the faith to work in whichever context it is that I
happen to find myself. In so doing I may well plod along
like a journeyman ball player in the lower minor leagues.
Then again I may happen to adorn it by virtue of one of
those rare combinations of gift and circumstance that land
certain persons in Cooperstown and others on pages 10 to
12 of the *Lutheran Book of Worship*, headlined "Lesser
Festivals and Commemorations."[46] In either case I become
one of those countless persons by whom tradition happens,
through whom the aptly named *regula fidei* is handed
along as a framework within which succeeding generations
of the baptized may struggle or exult, as the case may be.
Thus is exercised what G. K. Chesterton so neatly called
the "democracy of the dead," by which the Christian faith
is protected from the whims and predations of "that small
and arrogant oligarchy of those who merely happen to be
walking about."[47]

Surely then, one obvious and fundamental purpose of
the Church is to inculcate the tradition, or as one might be
required to phrase it in this spiritually agnostic culture, to
provide basic instruction in the rules of the game, i.e., cat-
echesis. Whether to infantly baptized insiders or to lapsed
and seeking outsiders, the news is passed, "Thus and so is
the Unknowable named and known among us, with consequences of yea and such for the manner in which we comprehend our world, describe our selves, conduct our lives,

and set our sights. We commend this to you. If for some reason you cannot receive it, propositionally, as a description of 'things as they really are,' then we urge you to receive it at least, regulatively, as the best and truest of all possible ways to describe 'things as they well might be.' We, smitten as you are from time to time by the dark night of the doubting soul, will continue in conversation not only with each other but also with the prophets, apostles, and saints of old to discern why and how those adjectives 'best and truest' apply."

Perhaps the reader has sensed the spirit of pastoral concession in the preceding lines. I myself tend to be unabashedly propositional in my orientation to the Christian faith. I am also convinced that there are times and occasions—the preaching moment, the consecration and distribution of the sacrament, the consoling of one newly bereaved, the absolving of a penitent—when to be less than propositional about that to which, or better, the One to Whom, one invites faith is to be wickedly delinquent in one's calling. But again, as St. Paul counsels the proud and confident faction of the Corinthian congregation (1 Cor 8:11–12), there are also times and occasions that call for concession. Surely one such occasion is the evangelizing or catechetical conversation with a North American neophyte who, with respect to the unseen things of God, is still mired, as it were, in the epistemological pits. To commend a regulative orientation as a point of departure for this person is surely, in the light of one's own propositional confidence in the promised working of the Holy Spirit, an acceptable concession.[48]

Then again, why limit the concessionary impulse to the neophyte? Why not extend it as well to that legion of lifelong confessors who these days are perhaps best described as the "would be faithful"? Staggered and confused by that daily barrage of competing truth claims to which they've been subjected for lo these many years, they find themselves slipping deeply into the same pits where the neophytes are thrashing about. As they join in the thrashing, many look back with wistful yearning to the good old days of youthful yore under stern old Pastor So-and-So, who, while he may have never cracked a smile during confirmation class, managed nonetheless to have left the wonderful if fleeting impression that it was all most certainly true. "Out of the depths have I cried to Thee, O Lord. Lord, hear my voice."

How the Rules Require the Gospel

Come to think of it, the very rules of the game require extending the concessionary impulse to whomever is in need of it. Paradoxically, this is the very reason for insisting that the rules must be observed.

Writing strictly out of my own tradition, here is what I mean. In Lutheran congregations the rules stipulate that the telling of the Christian faith be governed by a clearly delineated doctrinal framework to which both the pastor and the congregation itself are formally committed, the former by virtue of ordination vows, the latter by its constitution. This framework rests on a documentary foundation of the Holy Scriptures as "authoritative source and norm of proclamation, faith, and life," the ecumenical creeds, and the sixteenth century Lutheran confessions, especially the Augsburg Confession and the small catechism.

In passing I note that I would be thunderstruck if so much as a single member of the typical Lutheran congregation (I think again of Trinity; also of the parish I presently serve) could repeat the substance of this last sentence with any degree of precision. Indeed, some might be surprised to learn that such elaborately prescribed boundaries exist, let alone that their pastor pays careful attention to them. It may be that his doing so nonetheless produces effects that many are aware of and appreciate. Perhaps old-timers find comfort in the fact that notwithstanding all the novelty of recent decades—the green hymnbook, early communion for the children, women in the pulpit—they continue to hear most of old Pastor So-and-So's core verities when they go to church. Perhaps newcomers are glad for a certain strength of pastoral utterance that momentarily numbs the sense of Not Knowing which gnaws on their innards, a strength that produces fifteen, maybe twenty minutes of sweet sermonic relief from the miserable feeling that they and everyone else they know are bumbling helplessly and more or less pointlessly toward a future whose only certainty is the dead certainty of the grave.

But if in fact they do notice these things, then what they will have picked up is nothing more than the superficial consequence of their pastor's attention to the Lutheran rules.[49] At a much deeper level, imperceptible to those not involved week in and week out with sermon preparation, catechetical instruction, sickbed visits, and the like, the intention and (one prays) the effect of the pastor's confessional rule playing is to ensure that Trinity's members will continue week in and week out, if only for that Sunday morning hour of corporate liturgical gathering, to be told the Gospel, and nothing in its stead which is less, more, or other than the Gospel. I use "Gospel" for the moment in its phenomenological sense. What they are to be told is news from God which is not only good but entirely good; not a tired rehashing of an old, old story, but genuine news which is entirely good *for them*; entirely good for them also and especially in the specific circumstances of their epistemologically challenged North American condition.

But if what they are told is less than that; or if what they are told comes draped in all manner of iffy encumbrances (if you do this, if you believe that, if you manage somehow to accomplish the other), then what they are being told is not yet good or newsworthy enough to be called Gospel, and ought not under any circumstances to be passed off as such.

At heart, this is what the confessional rules are all about. The Gospel must be told, with nothing less, nothing more, and nothing other served in its place. Thus the famous Lutheran *solas—sola gratia, sola fide, sola scriptura—* which are shorthand for the proposal that Article IV of the Augsburg Confession rightly serves as the essential regulative principle not only for Lutherans but indeed for the whole Church. When read in this light, as a regulative principle, this article asserts that justification entirely for Christ's sake, received solely through faith and apart from works is in point of catholic fact (not sectarian fiat) the article on which the Church, itself formed by the Gospel, either stands or falls.[50]

Played out in the nitty gritty of ordinary human lives, this principle means that the Gospel has not yet been told to Trinity's parishioners if, when the telling is done, they find themselves sharing the condition of one Roger and various other denizens of a certain Camp Freedom, so poignantly described by Randall Balmer in his superb *Mine Eyes Have Seen the Glory.* Crippled by the iffy less-than-Gospel of their Wesleyan holiness tradition, they exhibit "a fragile veneer of confidence" beneath which seeps "an underlying, though largely unspoken, anxiety," "a sadness," "an uncertainty about the fate of their souls," and this even as they sing loudly about their Blessed Assurance.[51] To put it more precisely, the Gospel is not yet told at Trinity if, as at Camp Freedom, the telling is predicated on something the hearers must do. There the predication entails an avoidance of the pits of sin, as sin is defined by the holiness movement. At Trinity one cannot replace this with a requirement that hearers wriggle themselves free from the pits of epistemological pessimism and agnostic assumption and pump themselves full of propositional confidence about the content of the Christian faith.

Rather the Gospel, if it really is the Gospel, will enter the pits and catch hold of the hearers precisely where and as they presently find themselves, riddled with uncertainty, utterly tentative about any kind of assertion concerning the Things Deemed Unknowable. Precisely in that condition they will encounter it (if it is the Gospel) as good news. This is the rule, the heart and nub of that regulative doctrinal framework, received by tradition, anchored in Holy Scripture, to which pastor and congregation are formally committed. Undergirding this rule, and paradoxically required by it, is the assertion which opened this study, "The Word became flesh [i.e., entered the pits] and dwelt among us, full of grace and truth; and we have beheld his glory."

Says then the faithful, rule-observing pastor, "For your own sake, dear parishioners, none of this blithering nonsense about Jesus authorizing all species of religious observance. Given where you yourselves are, only Jesus himself will do!" So it is that the Gospel becomes, for pastor and parishioner alike, required speech.

The Required Gospel

I cannot pretend in the brief space here available to explore fully how the Gospel of Jesus Christ is Gospel for North American spiritual agnostics. What I must do is to outline a few salient features of that Gospel which those who preach to these agnostics will need to accent if the churches they populate are to become Church, actively embracing the purposes of the Church's Lord.

First, the Gospel, by its own testimony, is alien to us. Its origins lie beyond us (John 1:1; 1 Cor 2:6–7). It is God's Gospel, not, as the exegetical guild would commonly have it, the product of vivid first century imagination. Against this view stand the apostolic witnesses (1 Cor 15:3–8; Heb 1:2; 1 John 1:1–3), to say nothing of ordinary common sense.[52]

Second, being alien to us, we should expect the Gospel to sound alien; to be in fact that scandalous stumbling block to the Jews and folly to the Gentiles which St. Paul observes it to be (1 Cor 1:23).[53] As Lesslie Newbigin comments on

John 16, it "will be in the form of a contradiction of the
world's most fundamental beliefs."[54] Conversely, if what we
hear fits easily with our presuppositions and predilections,
we are not hearing the Gospel.

Third, the Gospel is news to us. It is not a demand from
us. It is not a stipulation of what we must do for God (the
word for that is law). It is rather an announcement of the
good things God has done for us in Jesus, and continues
consequently to do for us through the activity of Jesus'
Spirit in the present day proclamation of the Gospel and its
sacramental administration.[55] Because God does these
things constantly, the Gospel is constantly God's new and
good word to us, i.e., the Good News.

Fourth, above all, the Gospel is not a demand that we
exercise our freedom correctly by choosing Jesus and/or
the religion(s) centered on him over other available religious options. Quite dramatically to the contrary, it is the
announcement that God in his astounding mercy has exercised his freedom to choose us (John 15:16). His method of
choosing us is "the word of [Christ on] the cross" (1 Cor
1:18). This is a word, a deed, a person so alien and abhor-
rent that we *cannot* choose it for ourselves as a preferred
spiritual option.[56] If God thereby crushes our pride (1 Cor
1:29), he also makes it impossible for us to construe of faith
in Christ as a demand. It can only be a gift. The Gospel's
scandal is therefore of the Gospel's essence.

Fifth, pushing that last thought a step further: this alien
Word-Made-Crucified-Flesh whom we are obliged to abhor
(Isa 53:2–3; Mark 15:23–32) is the starkest manifestation
of God's fierce horror—his wrath, to use the traditional
word—over the arrogance with which we presume to find
our own way among religious and spiritual options. In this
arrogance we go so far as to reduce God himself, revealed
though he be through the word of the prophets and the
specifics of Israel's history, to the lowly category of mere
possibility, one among a host of other possibilities. Having

so reduced him, we then allow ourselves and each other to spurn or select him according to the dictates of personal taste and inclination. For his part, God is not amused.

Sixth, the cross therefore announces that God will be had by us and we by him on his terms, and his terms only, i.e., *solus Christus*. He will not allow us to pick and choose our own way out of the pits. Come to think of it, arrogant and presumptive choosing is the original sin (Genesis 3), to which God's preliminary response has been to exacerbate our arrogance, allowing us to get lost in a maze of ineffectual and putrid choices (Isa 6:9–10; Rom 1:18–25). What then is the spiritual agnosticism of North America if not a present manifestation of the wrath of God? So is that persistent pressure within North American churches to replace the apostolic scandal of Christ Crucified with a "chooser-friendly" tale of Jesus the Sage (see chapter 1).

Seventh, Christ Crucified is nonetheless *for* such as these, he is not against them. This is the Gospel, both good and new. There is no such thing as news that is fresher or better than this. This is why, strictly speaking, there is no other Gospel.

Eighth, again, the Gospel is not a demand for impossible certainty on our part with respect to the things of God.[57] Rather, the Gospel is the simple announcement that God, countermanding his own wrath in Christ Jesus, is utterly certain about loving us.

Ninth, this love is manifested in the fact that the road to the cross begins when Jesus, incarnate Son of God, becomes the friend of sinners. Indeed the very thing which gets him killed is that he dares continually to forgive the sin of such as these.[58] Sin includes doubt and uncertainty about the identity of his person and the character of his mission and witness. This too he forgives, as is apparent in the post-Easter restoration of Peter the Denier (John 21). Peter, come to think of it, is the epitome of what it means to get things wrong not only believingly, but also, at a deeper level, epistemologically. This is true not only in his career as a disciple (Matt 14:31; 16:22–23) but also in his apostleship (Acts 10; Galatians 2).

Tenth, two things stand out sharply in this example of Peter. One is the lifelong persistence of doubt and uncertainty despite the most intense exposure to the Gospel in the person of Jesus himself (to say nothing of the consequent outpouring of the Holy Spirit). The other is Christ's own boundless patience with the doubter.

Eleventh, the sin of Peter's doubt stems significantly from a faulty epistemology, as do the sins of the disciples' climactic defection, of Israel's rejection of Jesus, and of Rome's participation in this. When Jesus forgives these sins—and ours—he takes them into and upon himself.[59] This, at its deepest, is the mystery of the Gospel (2 Cor 5:21).[60] Jesus the Christ, now identified with us, is himself driven by God into the pitch-black pits of anguished confusion and horrible not-knowing with respect to the Things of God. Note the witness of Matthew and Mark to his final cry of dereliction.[61] That God raises Christ from the dead is therefore the promise that we too will be brought out of the pits into which God himself has driven us, within which he has also mercifully chosen to find us.

Twelfth, this promise is both confirmed and kept when Christ bestows the gift of the Holy Spirit (John 20), who alone makes it possible in the present age to use the language of faith in Christ with power and conviction (Acts 2).[62]

Thirteenth, this is also to say that only by the gift and the working of the Holy Spirit, active wherever the Gospel is preached and the sacraments are administered (Augsburg Confession V; cf. 1 Cor 12:3), can the Church begin to embrace its mission and fulfill its purpose of bearing witness to the grace and glory of God in Jesus Christ.[63]

Finally, the Gospel, at once utterly scandalous and riotously splendid in its newsy goodness, is God's ongoing response to the present dilemma of tongue-tied ministers and reluctant confessors. The Church's pastors therefore have nothing except the Gospel to say as they seek to respond to this same dilemma. Let them say it with joy and confidence, for "with God all things are possible." The rich can be saved, including those whose wealth consists of an overabundance of religious options. This means that postmodern camels can also be drawn through the needle's eye of the Church's confession; or so implies the Church's Lord (Matt 19:24–26).

Models (and Anti-Models) of the Gospel's Telling

I confess again that I write this account of the Gospel with feet firmly planted in the Lutheran tradition of its telling. Others, thinking out of other traditions, will surely want to discuss certain features of my account at greater length. For that thanks be to God; let the discussion begin. Only let the conversation center squarely on the critical question of precisely what the Gospel is. Too often that question is taken for granted, as in much recent ecumenical dialogue. Reading the reports, one frequently gets the feeling that pressures for amity have sped the interlocutors through matters that our forebears more wisely recognized as weighty and substantial. When it comes to the core of the Church's faith one dare not rush. It is it not immediately obvious how ancient accounts of the deeds, death, and resurrection of one Jesus of Nazareth can function as excellent, enlivening news for twenty-first century listeners. The matter needs to be thought through with care, and then thought through again and again until it can be told with integrity, fidelity, and passion. Failure to do this thinking leaves both theologian and preacher too widely open, especially these days, to the danger of peddling something which is patently not the Gospel.

After all, abroad in the land are approaches to the conflict between the culture's agnostic imperatives and the Church's faith and witness which, for agnostic hearers, are mostly bad news. Two in particular leap to mind. Both are widely popular. Each competes bitterly with the other. Neither relieves the hearer's doubt-stricken condition. Instead each serves to exacerbate it.

The first approach is endemic to much of North American evangelicalism and certainly to its fundamentalist wing. It calls on "true believers" to circle the Christian wagons and meet the culture's agnostic onslaught with a hard-edged "I'm right and you're not" certainty; a certainty as fragile as it is brittle, based as it is on an arbitrary and necessarily rigid adherence to this, that, or the other theory of Biblical inerrancy.[64] In some of its manifestations the approach seeks also to construct a "Christian" culture (with "Christian" antonymous to "secular," "Catholic," and "liberal Protestant"); a culture replete with bowdlerized simulacrums of the artifacts one encounters in the realm of the infidels—rock bands, movies, web sites, bookstores. In H. Richard Niebuhr's terms, this is "Christ against culture" weirdly combined with a new "Christ co-opting culture." Or so it seems.

That the term "evangelical" should have come to be so widely associated with this approach is odd in the extreme. The approach tends, after all, not only to contradict the Gospel in spirit but to diverge from it in fact. Its Jesus typically demands of his hearers from on high that they "accept him as their personal Savior" (the "or else!" always implied). But this is not the Jesus of Luke 15. By no stretch of the imagination is he the one who first empties and then humbles himself (Phil 2:7–8), the outrageously gracious Lord Christ who plunges into the cultural pits to make friends with the doubting, searching sinners who are wallowing there. He certainly does not save those sinners from the sin of choosing a preferred deity for themselves. Nor does he relieve them of the Sisyphean burden of having to find their own way up and out to the verities of God, moral or doctrinal. Instead he compounds the sin and also adds to the burden. To return to my earlier sports metaphor, this approach plays baseball by aiming the ball at the batter's head.

Worse still is the second approach, rampant in the Protestant mainline, which wants to invent a different game altogether and still call it baseball. Instead of waging war against the culture's agnostic impulse, it yields to it, chiefly through a process of deconstruction which strips the Gospel of its alien character as a word not of our own devising. This leaves one free to construct a "gospel" to one's own liking, and, beyond that, to remake a god in our present image, fashioned after our contemporary likeness. This appears to have been the approach adopted by the conference cited at the beginning of this chapter. One encounters it as well in any number of writers from the postmodern feminist perspective, of whom Beverly Harrison of Union Theological Seminary might be cited as an example. In her work she abandons altogether the term "Christ," so essential to the New Testament's Gospel, and speaks instead only of Jesus who, as she quickly gives the reader to understand, was surely not raised from the dead.[65]

Or take J. Edward Carothers, former head of the national missions agency of the United Methodist Church. In a courageous and honest book he makes the common mistake of confusing the culture's agnostic attitude toward the supernatural with an inability to entertain it even as possibility. This drives him to urge the promulgation of a Jesus recovered from burial beneath "dusty legends and myths," redeemer no longer but rather "our inspiration and guide."[66] The problem, of course, is that without these dusty "legends" about the one who swallowed sin, killed death, and subdued the wrath of God there is no such thing as a Gospel worthy of the term. Discarding them leaves human beings wallowing in their sins, bereft of honest hope for anything that is finally and utterly good. A theologian of this ilk may well object that there is no sin to wallow in, at least not in the classic Christian sense of something which offends God and provokes his wrath. Hope, he may say, is universal, for God saves all if indeed God saves any. The canny agnostic, listening in, will at this point ask "How do you know this?" Without that "stuff of legend" to fall back on the theologian now has nothing of demonstrable substance to say. He therefore has no choice but to leave the agnostic as haplessly stuck in the pits of Not Knowing as ever she was—the same pits, by the way, in which he himself is still woefully mired. Neither he nor she, of course, will dare to admit that God has had a hand in putting them where they are. This is the inescapable outcome of telling less or other than the apostles' scandal of Christ crucified.

Such an outcome is much less likely when the Gospel is handled obediently and explicated with care. Pastors who wish to minister seriously to agnostically stricken flocks will do precisely that. Obviously, this means much more than a mere mouthing of the mantra "Jesus died for you." As true as this is, it requires tough and determined questions: What does this mean? Why should this matter? To what end shall I repeat it?

In their efforts at understanding, pastors can these days turn for help and support to the splendid work of any number of contemporary theologians, widely scattered across denominational lines and confessional traditions. What these theologians hold in common is a passion for the Gospel, an abiding confidence in its truth, and a deep sensitivity to the cultural realities which it presently engages. They will certainly argue and disagree with each other as theologians always have and always will. No matter. Pastors who want to do their work well will pay them heed.

While this is not the place for a survey of worthy writers and sources of help, I mention two such sources, the one because it deserves to be better known, the other because it deserves to be more highly praised as the standard one aims for in both content and spirit of proclamation.

The first arises from the ongoing labors of my own

teachers, Robert W. Bertram and Edward H. Schroeder, systematic mainstays of the late Christ Seminary–Seminex (the institution that made a fleeting appearance in the wake of the Missouri Synod wars of the early '70s). Both are now retired, though theologically active. Together with Walter R. Bouman, newly retired from Trinity Seminary, Columbus, they began in the 1960s to blaze a trail for North American Lutherans in what Bouman, borrowing from Langdon Gilkey, has called "foundational theology," although Schroeder and Bertram prefer these days to call it "Crossings theology."[67]

Inspired by the mid-century German theologian, Werner Elert, foundational, or Crossings, theology drives its practitioners to sharpen their telling of the Gospel until it addresses, as countermanding good news, the deadliness that human beings continually encounter in their daily engagements with reality. Reality, of course, is in constant flux. Adolescence is one thing, old age another. The modern secular '60s have given way to today's postmodernity and its riotous "spirituality." Therefore the theologian, more so still the preacher, is constantly at work to pitch the Gospel's telling to that particular condition in which the hearer finds herself. One of shifting reality's unshifting constants is the pressing weight of divine expectation that hovers over every life like the dark and crackling cloud on Sinai. This theology therefore takes it for granted that no human condition can be adequately described, let alone addressed, until one has taken the enduring, accusatory function of the Law of God into account. Then and only then does the Gospel become as sweet and enlivening as God intends it to be. Such are the methods and approach which have shaped my own relating of the Gospel in the pages above. The second source, to be praised highly, is the work of the late Lesslie Newbigin, British Reformed pastor, missionary, theologian, and ecumenist. Newbigin's especial strength as a theological resource for North

American practitioners comes, less oddly than it will at first seem, from his having spent the great part of his career in India. There he was obliged, as good missionaries always are, to learn the conceptual ins and outs of another culture. He then had to identify those points of contact through which the Gospel could be told as God's genuinely and profoundly good news also for those who lived in that place, in light of that worldview, according to that specific set of culturally ingrained assumptions about "how things are." Good missionaries are required to cultivate the virtues of patience, sensitivity, and respect for one's hearers. They are also driven to be constantly aware of the Gospel's nature as a strange and alien Word which, however good one knows it to be, will be difficult and challenging to hear. Newbigin's work exudes both these features.

This is assuredly why Newbigin, more than any other thinker I have lately encountered, has been able to identify and address those points in the conceptual worldview of Great Britain and North America that are most likely to harden ears to the Gospel. Homegrown contenders against the false gospels of the right and the nongospels of the left tend as a rule to make their points loudly and let it go at that. The Lutherans Braaten and Jensen came to mind here, as do the Methodists Hauerwas and Willimon.[68] Newbigin probes more deeply than any of these to engage the epistemological assumptions on which both false and nongospels rest. He does this most fully in his masterful *The Gospel in a Pluralist Society*. At the heart of his argument are the following points: first, that when the Western world assumes it impossible to conceive of the Christian message as knowledge, i.e., as a truthful and dependable description of "how things really are," this assumption rests on a prior series of false assumptions about the nature of knowledge, particularly with respect to the relationship between knowledge and belief. Second: in recognizing this, the Church does not need to back away from its mission of bearing witness to the Gospel as truth which all human beings are to hear, nor dare it back away if it intends to be faithful to its Lord. Third, in bearing this witness the Church is obliged on the one hand to be faithful to the Gospel's scandalous particularity and on the other to learn how to tell of it in ways that will enable people at least to listen. Above all, says Newbigin, let the Church in obedience to its Lord and his Spirit recognize that the Gospel, told and honored as truth for all, is its gift to the world. Others have said this, of course, and are saying it still. Newbigin as a rule says it better, chiefly because of the way in which he says it. His particular virtue, unmatched in other writers of similar intent, is a meticulous fidelity not only to the content but to the spirit of the Gospel. In particular he understands the necessity of pastoral concession. As he tells of the one Lord, that crucified, risen, and ascended Jesus in whom God has acted graciously and with love for the salvation of the world, he does so in a way that is deeply faithful to this Lord's essential character as friend of sinners. He does not berate and badger his hearers, be they Indian or British or North American. Finding them enmeshed in their epistemological confusions, he addresses them gently and patiently, taking the time (as good missionaries do; as Jesus, the master missionary, surely did with his disciples) to equip them with the tools that will enable hearing to begin.

I therefore note with pleasure that Newbigin's work has drawn a core of disciples in North America, chiefly from Reformed and Presbyterian circles. These, like the Crossings theologians, are presently doing work that is well worth following (www.gocn.org). One of these theologians, George R. Hunsberger of Western Theological Seminary, made a comment several years ago that captures the spirit I have been describing. In his keynote address to a 1993 consultation of the Gospel and Our Culture Network (the name is borrowed from a Newbigin inspired movement in Great Britain), Hunsberger observed that the mistake is too commonly made of juxtaposing the terms "gospel" and "culture" in oppositional contrast. This happens when one fails to remember that the Gospel, proclaimed in the gathered community of the church, is being addressed to the encultured. It also happens when one forgets that the Gospel, precisely in its address, is creating something new, a cultural community which is marked both by the stamp of the natal culture and by the transforming, reshaping power of God's good news. "We are the community," he said,

> which has been grasped by the claim of the gospel, which has inaugurated us into a conversioning by which the assumptions and dispositions we share with our culture are being repatterned along the lines of new loyalties, visions, and commitments. But we are aware that we are neither so fully and finally shaped by that gospel nor so unique and distinct from the culture as we may have wanted to think.[69]

The brunt of these comments, of course, is directed at people (mainly pastors) who too easily fancy themselves as standing with the Gospel against the culture, as if they themselves were somehow beyond the culture's grasp. But the thought might just as easily be turned around. It might be directed, again at pastors, who fancy themselves preaching Sunday in and Sunday out to people who are standing with the culture and against the Gospel, as if these very people were somehow beyond the Gospel's grasp.

Such a presumption, of course, is arrogant nonsense. I hasten to confess myself too often guilty of it. Again and again I find myself obliged to heed the witness of St. Peter. As Lutherans speaking from the particularity of their tradition like to observe, where the Gospel is preached there the Spirit works faith in Christ; and where the Spirit works such faith, there you will find a human being who can only be described, paradoxically, as *simul iustus et peccator*—at once righteous and sinner; found by God to be wondrously true and faithful, and this even as the same God finds her unacceptably riddled with doubt.

Conclusion

There is much more, in other words, to the reluctant confessors and tongue-tied ministers of North American churches than meets the eye. Let their pastors remember this; let this be the starting point in the quest for loosened tongues.

Not that what meets the eye should be discounted. This is, after all, who they are: the epistemologically afflicted; people whose language rules reflect the agnostic anxieties of the culture that shapes their existence, defines their world, and exerts too strong a hold over the intuitive beliefs and implicit assumptions they operate with, not only "in the world" but also among themselves, within their own congregational communities.

But this too is what these same people are: they are the baptized, the shriven, the communing. They are hearers of sermons and (on occasion) students of Scripture. They are people, in other words, to whom God has spoken and continues to speak in and through the Gospel of Jesus Christ. They are therefore people to whom the Spirit of Christ has come. That same Spirit continues to be at work within them, opening ears, softening hearts, easing fears, calming doubts, instilling the conviction which lies at the core of the Church's faith, namely that Jesus Christ, crucified for them and risen, is their Lord, on whose grace and boundless mercy they can continue to rely.

Like Peter, these are people with whom Christ may be trusted to be endlessly patient as they struggle with their doubts and follies. Again like Peter, these are people whom Christ and his Spirit are determined to put to work in spite of their doubts and follies—or so we have reason to presume, with great confidence.

As we are about to see, the same Gospel we are required
to tell them requires us to expect that Christ will have his
way with them. Anything short of that expectation par-
takes of an heretical spirit. For the sake of the Gospel, it
must be rejected.

4

The Gospel as Promising Proclamation

The Doubting Faithful

Something marvelous and strange has just happened, as it typically does when the Gospel is put into play. In effect, the terms of the very question which has driven this essay to the present point have been shaken up and stood on their head.

I have been asking, "How does tongue-tied church become confessing Church?" "How do assemblies of agnostically oriented North Americans, excessively silent where words of the faith are concerned, turn into confessing, ministering manifestations of the one, holy, catholic, and apostolic Church which gladly lives, and also suffers and dies, for Jesus its Lord?" The form of this question implies that these assemblies are not yet what they ought to be. It also implies that until these assemblies become what they ought to be, the purposes their Lord has in mind for them are necessarily unmet.

But the Gospel itself insists that these are false implications drawn from a muddled, faithless question.

Within the New Testament one encounters this insistence most notably, though hardly exclusively, in the prelude to the Great Commission of Matthew 28. A striking prelude it is. The scene is a Galilean mountaintop. There the eleven have gone, obeying instructions relayed by the women to whom Jesus appeared on the morning of the resurrection (28:10). Now they see Jesus for themselves (28:17a). Upon seeing him they do as the women had done (28:9b), as indeed the wise men of Matthew's infancy narrative had been the first of all people to do (2:11); they worship him. Now comes a striking comment, one that sets these eleven apart from both women and wise men while at the same time identifying them irrevocably with every worshipping believer who has followed in their wake.

"But some doubted," Matthew writes (28:17b). The reader is left to guess what the substance of the doubt might be. Does it focus on whether this Jesus who stands before them is real? (See Luke 24:42–3 and John 20:27.) Or does it focus rather on the deeper matter of whether, resurrection notwithstanding, one dares accord this Jesus the worship that is rightly due to God alone? (See John 20:28.)

The point is that "some doubt." In so doing they stand on that mountaintop in precisely the same condition that afflicts North American Christians as they occupy their pews of a Sunday morning. North Americans wonder if they find themselves in the presence of mere fantasy or legend. They wonder, too, whether one is right to incorporate Jesus of Nazareth into one's conception of the divine reality. As with North Americans, so with the apostles. One reasonably expects at this point that Jesus will erupt in a blast of exasperation, as he once did with the deaf mute's father (Mark. 9:19). More reasonably still, one looks for him to fire the doubters from their apostleship and recruit more trusting (and therefore trustworthy) replacements from the same ranks that produced Matthias (Acts 1:15).

Wondrously and graciously, Jesus does neither. Instead he merely, and immediately, issues precisely the same set of commands to doubter and non-doubter alike. "Go." "Make disciples." "Baptize." "Teach." And so they do. The fact that three decades shy of two millenia later I occupy a pulpit from which I address some five hundred listeners Sunday in and Sunday out is itself living testimony that apostolic doubt is by no means an impassable barrier to apostolic witness and confession. Why this is so emerges in the final words of Matthew's account. "Lo, I am with you always, to the close of the age," says Jesus. By "age" he means the present age of doubt which he himself has entered and died at the hands of, an age when even those enlightened by Word and Spirit are obliged to "walk by faith and not by sight" and therefore to stumble, often badly. Yet that stumbling will not prevent this Lord and Christ from achieving his purposes in and through the stumblers, be these the apostles themselves or their latter day descendants. Such is the effective content of the promise, a promise vested with the authority of creation's author and therefore one of those words that does not return to its speaker with its intention unfulfilled (Isa 55:11). Feckless doubters, assembled, authorized, and commanded by Christ to confess him as Lord will make that confession in spite of their doubt—or their fecklessness. Christ's presence with them ensures this.

It therefore makes no sense to keep asking how church becomes Church, or how scandal-leery semi-agnostics can be turned into confessing, ministering agents of the Gospel. Instead the focus shifts to two other questions. First, how is it that Christ can be present these days among the semi-agnostics we know, love, and are? Second, how might it be, given Christ's presence among them, that these assemblies of the tongue-tied are already functioning as Church and accomplishing the purposes of their Lord?

To the first of these new questions the answer is plain. Jesus is present when and wherever the words that rightly tell of him are present. I say "rightly tell" because it is all too possible to tell of him wrongly, as we have seen. That this right telling and presence are at once contemporaneous and necessarily connected is underscored by the famous promise of Matthew 18:20, "Where two or three are gathered together in my name, there am I in the midst of them." These days, as always, the predicating "in my name" is fulfilled only when the name named by the gathered two or three or more belongs honestly and recognizably to the author of the promise, that is, to the Jesus encountered in apostolic testimony. Modified versions of this Jesus, gussied up in a pandering appeal to contemporary sensibilities, will not satisfy the promise's condition. After all, the Jesus they name is simply not the Jesus who made the promise in the first place. We do well to bear in mind that men and religious figures named Jesus are historically legion. Only one is the Christ, the Son of the Living God, and the Word made Flesh Who Dwelt among Us. Again we find a pressing reason for exercising diligence and care in the discerning of what and Whose the Gospel is.

Across North America's length and breadth are innumerable gatherings of two and three and often hundreds more that do happen authentically in Jesus' name. Within them the Gospel is preached and sacramentally enacted in recognizable conformity to the witness of the apostles and the historic confession of the Church catholic. Those gathered name Jesus as Lord. They acknowledge him to be the Christ. They worship him, in unity with his Father and the Holy Spirit, as the one God. It falls especially to those of us who preside over such gatherings to acknowledge these things cheerfully. Cheer is called for by the conviction that Christ, having kept the great promise to rise from the dead, is assuredly keeping the lesser yet still impressive promise to be present in the midst of gatherings precisely like these.

This merits underlining. The thing that properly commands our attention is not the gathering itself but the promise that attends the gathering. So Luther would quickly observe, and, well before him, St. Paul. Paul, of course, is the first to reflect on the gross discrepancy between the present, defining quality of the gathering promise and the prior quality of the ones gathered. "Not many of you were wise," he says to the fractious Corinthians, "or powerful or of noble birth; but God chose what is foolish, weak, low and despised, even things that are not. Boast not of yourselves, then, but of Christ Jesus who [alone] is our life, our wisdom, righteousness, sanctification, redemption" (1 Cor 1:26–30). Because of Christ "all things are yours: . . . life, death, the present, the future" (3:21–22). Throughout the Corinthian correspondence Paul astounds the reader by his proclivity to speak rhapsodically and with the highest expectation of a congregation that, in terms of its reported conduct, is a wretched embarrassment. Driving the rhapsody is Paul's utter regard for the transfiguring presence of Christ in the embarrassment's heart. "If anyone is in Christ, he or she is a new creation." This noted, he insists on taking his own advice to "regard no one from a human point of view" (2 Cor 5:16–17). Therefore he addresses them as saints (1 Cor 1:2) and foresees their guiltlessness (1 Cor 1:8), moral ragamuffins though he knows them to be (1 Corinthians 5–6). He reminds them of their future as judges of angels (1 Cor 6:3). He repeatedly calls them brothers. He assures them of his love (1 Cor 16:24). By contrast he heaps nothing but scorn on the better behaved Galatians. Christ is missing from that assembly. This is so because they have turned to "another gospel" (Gal 1:6).

If Corinthians merit praise and honor for Christ's sake, then so do the congregations we serve; presuming again that Christ is present in them, as indeed he is when we ourselves take the lead in proclaiming his Gospel to them. Some of these congregations will be strikingly vigorous and open in their confession of the faith. Certainly a few will be just as striking in the degree to which God's ministry, embodied in the mutual conversation and consolation of the faithful, is taking place within them. Somewhere in the land there are parishioners like the one I imagined in chapter two, from whose mouths the words of faith spill easily and accurately. I strongly suspect that the greater number of congregations—this is certainly true of Lutherans—are like the Trinity of my case study: tongue-tied, epistemologically afflicted, colored through and through with the agnostic presumptions and anxieties of their natal culture. In the final analysis, none of this matters. I say this with great care, keeping in mind that the final analysis is God's, not ours. But if Corinthian sinners can rightly be called saints, then North American agnostics can rightly be called the faithful. Indeed this is what they must be called so long as Christ is with them through the Gospel proclaimed in their gathered midst. It rests with their pastors to take the lead in calling them what are. This is a critical component in our own obedience to the Gospel. May this obedience be glad.

May it also be expectant. There is, after all, much more to Paul's move at Corinth (or ours in North America) than verbal chicanery, a praising of the naked emperor for his imaginary clothes. The saintliness Paul sees and lauds is, in the first place, Christ's. So is the faithfulness we properly praise. But what is Christ's is quickly catching, as the first disciples learned. However thickheaded and doubt-racked they be as they trail behind him through Galilee (Mark in particular takes pains to underscore this), the fact remains that they have left nets and tax booths behind in a primary act of faith, the faith itself engendered by the creating word of Christ's invitation to follow him. Amid all the "not getting it" which ensues, sometimes to Jesus' own exasperation—"O ye of little faith!"—one spots here and there the sprouts of faith still alive and new creation emerging. They may shriek in obtuse terror as waves shiver their boat; even so, they continue to trust Jesus enough to wake him, expecting that he'll somehow save them. Then comes that other night on the same lake, when Peter walks on water, if only for some seconds. So also with the Corinthians. However roundly Paul may score them for sinful self-absorption at their own common meals (1 Cor 11:17–22), he also calmly anticipates their saintly participation in a collection to buy food for saintly strangers (1 Cor 16:1–4). What he anticipates he gets (2 Cor 9:2). Christ's righteousness in them is real.

Pastors of North America's doubt-stricken flocks are obliged to anticipate nothing less of Christ's faithfulness. Like the righteousness, it is real. It is also productive, so that Christ keeping faith with us through the Gospel constantly iterated can be expected of Spirit-driven necessity to engender faith kept with him, however imperfectly, if only for some seconds. Before wringing our hands over the extent to which this responding faith is not apparent, it behooves us to look carefully for signs that it is there, and working. The absence of open confession does not mean that no confession is happening at all. A lack of fluent conversation and consolation among the brothers and sisters does not equate with a total breakdown in the evangelical ministrations of the flock, one member to another. The chore is to poke around with eyes and ears open for those signs of lively faith that are present, and, on spotting them, to draw attention to them, to encourage them, to celebrate them, to thank God for them. As with broken sidewalks, so with agnostic congregations; one looks for the growth in nooks, crannies, and cracks. One does well to look with confidence. If God's crab grass will not be denied, still less will God's Gospel be. Jesus himself teaches us to anticipate this with his comments about seeds growing secretly and leaven tucked away in lumps of dough.

This is the lesson I finally learned at Trinity. After spending too much time in pained objection to what I was not seeing or hearing in that congregation, I began to pay attention instead to what was there. What drove me to do so more than anything was the weekly imperative to preach a Gospel that insisted on naming as saints the very people who sat in front of me, trapped though they were in their agnostic afflictions. Inevitably I looked for signs of the

saintliness and found them. A woman speaks reverently of
her mother's quiet faith the night their house burned down.
Another woman chastises me gently for having suspended
the sacrament on a Sunday when I was away without an
ordained stand-in to call on. She understands the reason
for the suspension, but she missed too badly that weekly
connection with her Lord in the sacrament. A man atypi-
cally sets aside his chagrin after a nasty internal argument
because "it's the Christian thing to do." Later the chagrin
resurfaces, but no matter. If only for a week or two he has
walked on the waves.

Amid thickets of tongue-tied doubt I start to see sprouts
of confession. A teenaged boy invites a classmate to
church; the whole family appears. Others, trickling in, are
welcomed with warmth and encouraged to stay. I notice
the joy at baptisms. I hear of gingerly attempts to draw
lapsed family members back to church. All of this happens
very quietly, even secretively. The point is, it does happen.
Is Christ named in the happening? Probably not. But as a
wise man eventually teaches me, the failure to name is not
yet a failure to confess.

His name is Andy. I will let it go at that, though I don't
imagine he'd mind overly much were to I to use his last
name too. He was then in his early 50s, the owner of a
small, successful metal-working business. Andy was one of
those few quiet pillars that smaller congregations habitually rely on for their survival. I had therefore asked him one
evening to sit with me and a handful of others to talk about
the defining purpose of the major building project the congregation was about to embark on.

As usual I was on my pastor's high horse, pushing, prod-
ding, and poking with all manner of questions about the
connections between congregation and Church, between
organizational objective and confessional purpose. "How,"
said I, "does this building serve the purposes that God has
in mind for a Christian congregation? Do we for our part

believe in those purposes, especially as they find their focus in the Gospel of Jesus Christ? Do we accept that what we do in this building project is somehow to serve Christ's intention that we be his witnesses in this particular corner of the world, and if so, how is this to happen? Do we build primarily to look after ourselves or to serve others? If others, do we know what those others are looking for, and is that what we either have or want to offer?" In the ensuing conversation I heard things I had not been hearing, at least not openly, in the years prior: how those present were fiercely jealous of their identity as a Christian congregation; how the Gospel was of profound importance to them; how its scandalous particularity was seen as its strength and was not to be downplayed (in blue collar terms, "we can't cut the guts out of the faith"). Somebody, I recall, poked back at my poking by warning against facile distinctions between God's purposes and our purposes, as if the two could be easily separated. It struck me in that moment as a useful caution, and does so still. At one point the discussion turned to the building's potential role as a drawing card for newcomers. All agreed that the congregation was anxious for new members and fresh energies. One or two opined that it was nonetheless impossible to guess what church-shopping newcomers might want, leaving the congregation with the sole and happy option of building for its own needs. Now Andy broke in, a little impatiently, somewhat brusquely. "Of course we know what newcomers are looking for," he said. "They're looking for a pretty building. It's not what they need, but it's what they're looking for. So here's what we do. We bait the hook with a pretty building, and then we reel them in. Once they're here they'll eventually find the prize that's waiting for them in this place. All the rest of us have found it. We know we have. The prize is Christ."

Coming from a postmodern ex-Catholic Lutheran male with remnants of working-class calluses on his hands, this is tantamount to Peter's confession at Caesaraea Philippi.

In this matter of how postmodernists confess the faith, Andy remains my primary teacher. He reminds me in the first place of the manner in which their confessing typically happens: quietly; surreptitiously; more often than not, collectively. I could not and cannot imagine Andy talking to his workers about his faith in Jesus. I can imagine that when he invites those workers to the annual picnic of Trinity's Men's Club he does so with the niggling hope that this time around one of them might be pleased enough to come back for another look on Sunday, thus bumping into the Jesus Andy trusts. Again, I doubt that Andy would care to echo Peter's assertion about salvation in no other name. Alive as he is to post-Constantinian reality, I suspect its implications trouble him badly enough that he tries hard not to think about them. I'm quite certain even so that Andy knows the name in which his own salvation lies, and will hardly be surprised when others find in Christ the same hope he has tasted for himself. All this shapes his approach and style as a confessor. He bears his witness not as the rugged, risk-taking individual he otherwise is, but as a member of the group. He relies on the congregation— more pointedly, perhaps, on the congregation's pastor—to make the confession for him. He announces that Jesus is Lord not through words but through deeds, beginning with the deed of making sure that he's sitting next to his wife in the favored pew every Sunday. Beyond that comes the generous weekly contribution to the offering plate and the quiet participation in selected congregational programs and activities, to a few of which he occasionally lends his unassuming yet richly effective leadership. For him the steady fact of Trinity itself is how Jesus gets confessed. His faithfulness is to know the prize, the gift of gifts that Trinity offers to those who find themselves "reeled in." The prize is none other than his Lord, the one who has promised to be there in the gathered midst of the two or three, or in Trinity's case, the weekly hundred. Like so many other

North American Lutherans, Andy will hardly ever speak of him. Even so he will certainly do his part to proclaim him—or more accurately, to ensure his proclamation. And he will wish his pastor to let him be content with that.

A piety deeply imbedded in the broad tradition of American Protestant Christianity will call this a cop-out on Andy's part. I mean that piety which takes its cue from Acts 1:8, where it insists that the sentence "You shall be my witnesses" be read in the imperative mood, as an injunction not to a group but to a set of individuals who happen coincidentally to be standing in the same place at the same time. In this light, each and every believer is dominically obliged to challenge the culture's proscription of explicit Christian speech by identifying herself openly as a Christian (not merely as a church member), by speaking freely of her Lord and her faith to others, and above all by inviting the ignorant or the disbelieving to come to Christ. Andy fails the test of this piety. So do the majority of North American Christians. Pastors who have felt its influence in the formation of their own operative pieties will rue this. They will also feel duty-bound to correct it. In embarking on this project they will be sorely tempted to identify the failure to "witness" as a deficiency, a signal of insufficient believing or of poor and cowardly faith.

Such pastors, and I have been one of them, need to resist this temptation. Otherwise they risk the sin of burdening consciences unnecessarily, without scriptural warrant. The logic that drives the piety may seem compelling—if I really believe that Jesus is Lord, then I will have no qualms about saying that Jesus is Lord as I surely ought to and will want to. Closer examination suggests that the piety itself may be rooted more deeply in the theological and cultural assumptions of eighteenth century New England than in the expectations of the New Testament.[70] It is hardly news that North Americans accentuate both rights and responsibilities of the individual over those of the group; but one has to have spent time outside North America to grasp that our instinct to do this is not only strong, it is also peculiar. Furthermore, one has to have taught the Bible in a third world setting to perceive how strikingly this emphasis on the individual has skewed our understanding of the Word, to the point in some cases of rendering it obscure.

When North Americans hear the famous charge to "let your light so shine before others" (Matt 5:16) they assume unthinkingly that Jesus, like George Bush, has in mind a thousand points of light, or as many more of these as there are baptized and/or believing Christian persons. In so assuming they fail to notice that the "you" of the sentence is a plural "you," nor do they (nor can they?) consider the possibility that the "you" is not only plural but also collective. This possibility is certainly suggested by the fact that Jesus addresses this charge (as well as his prior comment about the salt) to a *group* of disciples, culled from the crowd and arranged on the hill before him (Matt 4:18–21; 5:1). The subsequent ecclesiological emphases of Matthew's Gospel underscore this possibility.

In other words, the point of light is not the individual believer but the individual gathering of believers. It is the church or congregation, the two or three or twenty or three hundred in whose midst is Andy's prize, the same Christ who, in John's testimony, identifies himself as the Light of the world (John 8:12). If the points of light be a thousand, that is because there are a thousand churches out there, twinkling away in the world's darkness. Such seems to be the suggestion also of the rest of the New Testament. Strikingly, Paul nowhere speaks of an individual obligation to hit the streets as a witness to Jesus, nor even to tell one's neighbor about him. According to Paul only a few are adorned with gifts to be front-line missionaries, a.k.a. apostles (1 Cor 12:28–30; also Eph 4:11–12, notable for its distinction between persons with gifts of proclamation and the rest of the saints). What matters far more to Paul is the

character and conduct of the group, and whether this conforms to the character of Christ. "Have this mind among
you which is yours in Christ Jesus" (Phil 2:5).

This concern is even stronger in John, who takes Paul a
step further by drawing an explicit connection between the
group's character and its witness to unbelievers (John
17:20–23). In the book of Revelation the points of light, or
to use its term, the lampstands, are seven, one for each of
the seven churches of Asia (Rev 1:20). These, not the individuals who comprise them, are the witnessing, confessing
entities through whom others come to believe that Jesus is
"the first and the last and living one" who died and is "alive
forevermore," who "holds the keys of Death and Hades"
(Rev 1:17–18). It is, one recalls, through the collective witness of his fellows that Thomas hears of the resurrection;
and only within their subsequent assembly around Jesus is
he brought at last to the ultimate Christian confession, "My
Lord and my God" (John 20:24–28).

Or so it seems. I acknowledge that the matter is more
nuanced than I am making it out to be and requires much
closer examination that is beyond this discussion. Even so,
we have surely seen enough to say this much fairly: it is not
nearly so obvious as imbedded pieties suggest that the
Church's pastors are obliged to hammer away at the
Church's Andys in an effort to get them speaking about
their faith. The supposition that every Christian is obliged
to make a verbal and public witness is just that: a supposition, by no means beyond argument and therefore potentially dangerous. Andy's Lord, after all, is not likely to be at
all pleased should Andy's pastor start hanging unnecessary
millstones around Andy's neck. He will urge in fact that the
millstone be transferred immediately to the pastor's neck
(Matt 18:6). Where the majority of our parishioners is concerned, the piety of individual verbal witnessing is precisely such a millstone. Even more so is the guilt which it
inevitably induces. The evidence in favor of the piety needs

to be much stronger than it is before pastors begin imposing it. It is by no means certain that Christ demands it.

At the same time this much is certain: such a demand
of Christ's cannot, by any stretch of the text, be extracted
from Acts 1:8. Again, the "you," subject of both sentence
and verse, is plural. Again, the words are addressed to apostles (not disciples as in Matt 28; see Acts 1:2); as we have
already noted, Paul makes it plain that not all are apostles,
but only a very few. But what carries this argument above
all is the mood of the sentence, not only its grammatical
mood but the air which pervades the passage as a whole.
"You shall receive power when the Holy Spirit comes upon
you, and you shall be my witnesses. . . ." This is an indicative statement. It is not the imperative that North
American hearers insist on making it out to be. It is
patently not a command. It is wildly a promise. Exactly
how wild is seen in the subsequent chapter when the Holy
Spirit, blowing where the Holy Spirit wills, turns the craven
denier into the rock-solid confessor and makes polyglot lin-
guists out of Galilean yahoos. Throughout the book of Acts
the real Witness and the true Confessor is this same Holy
Spirit. So also in the Pauline corpus, which seethes and
bubbles with the same idea (for example, 1 Cor 2:12–13;
12:3; Rom 8:15–17). John, too, underscores this point,
especially in the final discourse in the upper room
(16:12–15) but also in the Johannine Pentecost of 20:22
that, significantly, precedes the disciples' witness to Thomas.

In Matthew's Gospel Pentecost is implied. What implies
it is that absence of a pause between the acknowledgment
of the disciples' doubt and the authorizing command of
Jesus who sees their doubt. This, of course, is the same
Jesus who knows what it is to be led by the Spirit (Matt
4:1). He also knows how, in the Spirit, one overcomes the
severest temptations to doubt by remembering the Word
and then employing it, thereby putting it into doubt-defying
play (4:2–11). Assuredly he to whom "all authority in heaven

and on earth has been given" (28:18) now authorizes the Spirit who once led him to lead his doubting disciples. Therefore he is able to say "Go," knowing they will go. Therefore he says "make disciples," knowing that in their Spirit-led baptizing and teaching they will remember and employ the Word that does just that. Doubt him they may. Confess him they will. Jesus, for one, has no doubt about this.

And if we honor and obey him and trust his judgment, then neither will we doubt that confessing is getting done by, and through, the doubters who face us from the pews Sunday after Sunday. Agnostically stricken they surely are, too many of them excessively obedient to the postmodern demand that they know no truth, too many bucking at the scandal of a Jesus who is the Truth and insists on being proclaimed as nothing less than the Truth. Yet these same doubters are also rightly called the faithful. Their steady presence in those pews testifies to that. Baptized they are, and also regularly exposed to the Gospel. This is the Word that sets Christ, the crucified and risen one, in their midst. It therefore counters the wrath of their condition. It sets aside God's objection to the sin of their doubt. It gives entrée to the Spirit that vivifies Christ's new creation. It generates trust in Jesus. It gently and graciously seduces them into loving the very God and Lord they claim not to know.

This Word teems with promise. One piece of the promise is that these, the doubting faithful, are not keeping the promise to themselves but are getting it out and making it known. Someway, somehow. If not by shouting it, then by leaking it. If not through confident outbursts of individual testimony, then through the simple, undeniable fact of their life together as a Christian congregation. Together they worship and pray and share their common burdens. They also drink their coffee and eat their potluck dinners, they collect clothing for the homeless and foodstuffs for the local soup kitchen. They maintain their property, they sing in their choirs, they run their Sunday School, they support

a missionary. Above all they throw open their doors on
Sunday morning to any and all out there who might chance
to stumble in. All this they do in the name of Jesus.
Someone calls him their prize, and so he is. Almost all of
them know it. You can see it in their eyes as they kneel at
the table; you can hear it in their voices on those rare occasions when the pastor picks a hymn they really like to sing.

Among themselves they may not speak of Jesus much.
It makes them feel funny. They're not the experts, they
feel, and they know the rules about not imposing their private religious views on other people. If you ask them about
this, they'll look sheepish and one or two will shuffle their
feet until at last some crusty old codger points out—as if for
the first time; the way crusty old codgers are wont to do—
that this is what we've got a pastor for, and why we pay
him, to talk about Jesus for us. Come to think of it, there's
something very true about that. And if the pastor does what
the pastor is paid to do, then Jesus is there, as he has
promised to be; and Jesus' Spirit is with them.

So the little flock lives on as a point of Christ's light,
twinkling away in the chilly, doubt-ridden gloom of the
land it inhabits. Call it what it is: the miracle of the doubting faithful; or even better, the marvel of the faithful agnostics who manage in spite of themselves to keep on
confessing that Jesus is Lord.

This too should be added: God, looking on as he did at
Jesus' baptism or on the Mount of Transfiguration, is these days
deeply pleased. In the faithfulness of his Son to those people,
he is finding their faithfulness to him. This is the Gospel.

Coda

Since the days of the apostles most Christian assemblies
have made it their regular habit to pray the Lord's Prayer.
Most North American assemblies of most Christian stripes
still do, every Sunday. Lately it is fashionable for churches
with "seeker friendliness" on their minds to speak snidely

of the habit—why, I know not. How rightly to pray is one of the first things seekers will want to learn. Who better to teach them than the Lord Jesus himself? And if their silly guides would only step out of his way, our Lord Jesus would happily grant those seekers the great privilege of joining the Church of every time and every place in praying, among other things, "Thy will be done on earth as it is in heaven."

Addressed as this is on Jesus' authority to "our Father in heaven," it is a blessed thing to ask for. Luther makes this plain with the terseness marvelously characteristic of his Small Catechism where he writes, "The good and gracious will of God is done even without our prayer. But we pray in this petition that it will be done also among us."

I learned this as an eighth-grade confirmand. I had to get to the seminary before I started to comprehend what Luther was driving at. It took an Episcopalian, Robert Farrar Capon, to open my eyes. In *Hunting the Divine Fox*, Capon tackles the concept of the "will of God." He observes that we think of it habitually in hard Anglo-Saxon terms, as that which requires of us the stiff upper lip, the shoulders squared, the daily dose of castor oil and some good Teutonic discipline. In this we err. Why not think of it instead—Scripture surely invites this—in warm, romantic, Mediterranean terms; as the will of the lover for the one loved, as in the Song of Solomon. God's will for us is, pre-eminently, God's desire for us. It is also what God wants for us. It is therefore "good and gracious." It is done, as lovers do it, delightfully, surprisingly, before we get around to asking for it, "even without our prayer." But in loving back we let it be known that we want what we are getting. Let it be done, we say, "also among us."[71]

Of the countless things God wants for us, none is greater or more pressing than the yearning he continues to express and effect in Jesus. "[God] desires all people to be saved and to come to the knowledge of the truth" writes Paul, or perchance the Deutero-Paulinist (1 Tim 2:4, RSV).

Here, as everywhere in the New Testament, "the truth" is no mere idea or mindset, nor even the best of all possible takes on reality. It is finally a person. It is the Jesus who identifies himself as way, truth, and life, and who announces that "I, when I am lifted up from the earth, will draw all people to myself" (John 12:32). This drawing of persons to Jesus is above all else God's good and gracious will, immediate and pressing. Seekers need to know this. They certainly ought to be taught to pray for it. The fact that they are already seekers is a signal that Luther had it exactly right: God's will is done, his desires effected, even without our prayer.

Seekers either stream or stumble into churches because the rumor is still abroad in the land that in such places there might be something worth finding. Our postmodern circumstances have not squelched the rumor. If anything, they have magnified it by aggravating doubt and with it the ache to know that both prompts and accompanies our sinful condition, as it has from the beginning. I suggested in the previous chapter that this aggravation of doubt is itself a work of God. It is an alien work, to be sure, of itself unhappy; not the sort of thing one might expect of a God called good. Yet, because of its inextricable link to the pursuing of rumors, one dares to see in it too the desires of God at play. No one asked for it. We did not pray for it. It happens anyway.

As do the rumors. They too happen anyway, even without our prayer. I have in mind here the good rumors, good because they are useful and true and have the effect, ultimately, of fulfilling Jesus' intent. Through them people continue to be drawn to him, encountering him in his present condition of having been twice lifted up, first as the one who was crucified for all and then as the one who is Lord of all, to whom "all authority . . . has been given." In John's Gospel this distinction in liftings is somewhat arbitrary. Both are compressed into the single event at Golgotha, to the end that we see and understand: Jesus is the authoritative Lord because he has been crucified, and he is crucified because, from the beginning, he is the one and only Lord who does what all other lords, kings, and ruling types are supposed to do only they don't, which is to save their people, and if necessary at their own lordly expense.

I have been grappling in this essay with the question of how it is that the rumors are out there in the public consciousness of post-Constantinian North America. Driving my reflections has been the observation that those charged with spreading the rumors, members of North America's churches, are for the most part wretchedly reluctant to do so; so reluctant, in fact, that they can scarcely stand to bat the rumor back and forth among themselves. I have been casting the question in terms familiar to my own Lutheran tradition, how is Jesus getting confessed? I might just as well have been asking it in terms more digestible to those of other traditions, how is Jesus being witnessed to? With this has come another related and entangled question, how are North American churches doing the one thing above all others that the Church is supposed to do, which is to make that confession and bear that witness about Jesus their Lord? How indeed are they going to do it when the words of which rumors, confessions, and testimonies so necessarily consist are so noticeably absent from the mouths of those to whom this rumor, confession, and testimony has been entrusted?

An answer: they do it and will continue to do it even without our prayer. Confession happens and will happen because God wants it to happen. If the rumor about Jesus is not shouted then the rumor will be leaked; and it will be leaked in and through the collective behavior of those who are already somehow believing it. They sit in their pews Sunday after Sunday, and we their pastors talk to them about it; though we, if we are doing what we must do, are talking about it as much more than a rumor. We are presenting it instead as Gospel. We are picking up that hoary account (Carothers' old legend) of a dead Jew, now living, and we are pummeling it into hearers' ears not as the old, old story, still less as an old-time religion, but as news: today's surprising announcement of something lavishly good that is coming to them from God, unaccountably, in and through Jesus. When we do this the rumors begin. They ooze, flow—on occasion run—in ways we cannot hope to track or describe. But we are the primary source of them. We may as well acknowledge it. We do well in fact to own up to it. To be mongers-in-chief of the Jesus rumor: that—nothing else—is our calling.

The rumor will spread. Let there be no doubt about this. I return to an ancient axiom and offer it up again for my colleagues' consideration: if the Gospel is preached then confession will happen and witness will be borne to the Lord Jesus Christ who stands so graciously at the heart of that Gospel (see again Isa 55:11; compare Mark 13:11). It will happen, why? Because God wants it to happen and will make it happen, even without our prayer. "Faith comes by what is heard, and what is heard comes by the preaching of Christ" (Rom 10:17). Paul casts his verb in the indicative mood, and we should take this seriously. James Nestingen of Luther Seminary has written that the Gospel is "performative."[72] It causes the faith it seeks. With faith come behavioral consequences, and those consequences are the confession.

We will want as pastors to give close attention to habits of thought and expectation that impede the faith and confession of those we preach to. I have tried to do that in this essay. We are obliged to understand these habits as well as we can so that the Gospel we preach can address them squarely and have its way with them. We are also obliged, with Jesus, to be impatient with "little faith" and to point out as vividly as Paul does the often gaping discrepancies between faith and conduct. Meek and timid confession is not something to accept. While we rightly thank God for the accidental witness of the faithful, we are not to praise the doubters for witnessing by accident. The doubters and the faithful are one and the same, as we have seen. It falls to us to challenge the doubt, to call it into continual question, to drown it if possible in a torrent of our own words about Jesus.

We face the task as well of teaching the intentional use of Christian language; of training tongues to wrap themselves around forbidden words, to string them together in keeping with the rules of Christian grammar and syntax, and then to cut loose with them, appropriately and effectively, on hitherto forbidden turf. This requires much closer attention and greater diligence than I for one have been giving it. In the stream of junk mail that flows across my desk I find little sign that organizers of conferences and continuing education programs are paying attention to it either. I point to this as a matter that could use some sustained study, not only by pastors, but also by scholars.

There is finally one other matter that good pastors of postmodern flocks will attend to, with incessant care. We will as often as possible clamp shut our own mouths and assume the position of those hearers in the pews, waiting with strained ears to catch what God in the Holy Gospel is telling us. After all, we not only preach to the postmodern, we are the postmodern. Our ability to recognize the anxieties of those we minister to stems in huge part from the fact that we find them in ourselves. Confession of sin precedes confession of faith. Be it known that I am Peter, sinking below the surface of the lake. I am also Thomas, scoffing at the prospect that Jesus is risen. I get up on Sunday morning, charged by the Lord Christ to go and have another crack at making disciples, and I find myself grouped, invariably, among the disciples who doubted. So persistent is the doubt that I too am rightly called agnostic. Thus the Gospel is for me, for us; the Gospel of Christ, entering the gloomy pits of our own not knowing to raise us up, with him, to clarity and confidence. Let Christ be dinned into our ears by those we trust to tell of him faithfully and well, whether we find them in the books they write or among the colleagues with whom we gather in our own versions of the mutual conversation and consolation of the faithful. Let the bread be placed in our mouths and the cup lifted to our lips by hands other than our own, the accompanying words uttered by someone else who, believing them, thereby invites us, again, into the circle of faith, faith that clings against all reason to astounding, unthinkable words, "The body of Christ, given *for you.* The blood of Christ, shed *for you.*"

We will not propagate the rumor until we believe the rumor. We will not shout the Gospel from our pulpits until it has been shouted into our hearts. Therefore we pray, "thy will be done." We ask in this petition that the fierce and burning desires of God in Christ, salvifically active even without our prayer, will have their way with us.

Epilogue
A Personal Confession

Cleveland, Ohio (still). Fourth Week of Lent, 2000, in the thickness of the busiest piece of the parish pastor's year—

Since I began this almost a year ago, the words have flowed in a torrent. No, not the words of this essay, which have oozed like mud. I mean rather the words that the Word made Flesh has given me to utter, the words this essay is all about. I've been gushing them from my mouth because that's my job. It's what I'm paid for. I can think of some cranky old rams in my current flock who will be more than happy to remind me of that. Most of the time I don't need their reminders. I blurt out the words because they're great words to say. I blurt them out too because I believe them— mostly, and most of the time. Here and there this year I've endured a dark night of the soul, though never so dark as the one Peter endured the night the cock crowed, nor even so dark as ones I endured ten years ago. The pay in Cleveland beats the pay in New England, and that may have something to do with it. I'm also getting older, and either wiser or more set in my ways, and I'm also beyond that stage when a person still wonders whether there isn't something else he ought to be doing with his life, or she with hers. That may have something to do with it, too.

But the greater part of it, by far, is that I do love the words. I love them more than I used to; and the more I use them the more I love them. "Gospel" really is a tepid locution. I think that more strongly now than I did a year ago. When rightly used the words are not merely good, they're Tony the Tiger "great." When rightly used, the words aren't simply news, they're a thunderclap of joy beyond belief, only somehow, by a power greater than the force of their own incredulity, some hearers do wind up believing them (*veni creator Spiritus!*). I've seen it again in some shining eyes this year. I've seen it too in some feats of incredible courage, people clinging to hope when, humanly speaking, they ought to be in despair, or people daring to tell truths that typically kill the teller, but they tell them anyway. Deep down they're rolling the dice on the proposition that since their truth killed Jesus, they themselves can survive the telling of it. Rolling the dice is how the doubting faithful do their believing. It's how postmodernists "walk by faith and not by sight."

I wish I could say that I've always used the words rightly this year. I certainly haven't. I try to keep my eye cocked on the rules for using them, but sometimes the rush to crank out the next sermon has been too desperate. In any case, how in eighteen pulpited minutes do you begin to use the words rightly for all those people in all those circumstances— each and all of them staring at you in the hope that something you say will touch a particular condition, and heal it, and liven them up? I don't have the answer for that one. So I stand up and gush and blurt. Bumbling into that hospital room without a clue as to what I'm about to find, I find it, and then I improvise on the spot. I do that fairly well these days, but not always well. Practice doesn't make perfect, it only makes better. All the practice in the world will not keep the proclaimer from falling flat on her face from time to time, as Peter discovered at Antioch.

Still, this I believe—mostly; most of the time. I believe that somehow through me Christ has been busy feeding his

flock. I believe this not because I'm embarked on a postmodern project of defining my own reality, but because
Christ has graciously told me to believe it. Sure, they've
gotten milk sometimes when they needed meat, and vice
versa. Worse, they've too often found pebbles mixed with
the bread they asked for. But bread there has been, and
they are eating. The sign is that they keep coming, Sunday
after Sunday, to get more. The sign is that they've been
working hard to keep their church tempting to outsiders
because they really do care, collectively, about the Church's
confession; and it makes them very happy when tongues
besides their own start waggling the word that Jesus is Lord.
The sign is the strength of their response to the liturgy's
final word, "Go in peace! Serve the Lord!" And that's precisely what many of them attempt to do in those nooks and
crannies of their weekly sojourns. Or so they tell me.
Because they're middle-class North American Lutherans
they do it quietly, surreptitiously even. Never perfectly, or
even well. But they do it. And Christ in his mercy is busy
using them for his purposes, as he has been using me.

I will continue as I have to do my work with joy. I wish
the same for all my colleagues, but especially the younger
ones. I think in particular of the pastor out there in
Buzzard's Beak, whoever he or she may be. You know that
barrage of messages you've been getting about the poverty
and foolishness of your calling? To hell with them—literally.
Listen instead to your Lord Jesus Christ. The work you are
doing on his behalf is profoundly important and wondrously good. Do it gladly. Do it well. Attend with unrelenting care to how you tell the Gospel. Then wait for the taste
of joy. By the grace of God it will come.

I will pray for you. You pray for me. *Soli deo gloria!*

Notes

Chapter 1:
The Gospel as Scandal

1. For the concept of "indwelling," see Lesslie Newbigin, *Truth To Tell* (Grand Rapids: Wm. B. Eerdmans Publishing Co., 1991) 45–6.

2. A note on present usage: Church, uppercase "C," designates the entity confessed in the creed as "one, holy, catholic, and apostolic." The word in lower case, "church," will typically substitute for "congregation."

3. See Douglas John Hall, *The End of Christendom and the Future of Christianity* (Christian Mission and Modern Culture Series, Harrisburg, PA: Trinity Press International, 1997) 1–18; Stanley Hauerwas and William H. Willimon, *Resident Aliens: Life in the Christian Colony* (Nashville: Abingdon Press, 1989). I am choosing to follow these writers in using the term in its sociopolitical sense as "the Christian world" versus, say, "the Muslim world." The word can also serve as a theological construct denoting the totality of hearts in which Christ holds sway. In this latter sense, of course, Christendom continues unabated.

4. May Lamberton Becker, "How This Book Came to be Written," introduction to *Pride and Prejudice*, by Jane Austen

(Cleveland and New York: The World Publishing Company, 1946), 5.

5. Francis Fukuyama, "The Great Disruption: Human Nature and the Reconstitution of Social Order," *Atlantic* 283 (May 1999) 55–80.

6. See *The Secular City* (Cox), *Naming the Whirlwind* (Gilkey), *A Rumor of Angels* (Berger), and *The Naked Public Square* (Neuhaus). For publication details, see References Cited.

7. Harvey Cox, "The Market as God: Living in the New Dispensation," *Atlantic* 283 (March 1999) 18–23.

8. Carl E. Braaten, "The Gospel for a Neopagan Culture," in Carl E. Braaten and Robert W. Jenson, eds., *Either Or: The Gospel or Neopaganism* (Grand Rapids: Wm. B. Eerdmans Publishing Co., 1995) 9–10.

9. *No Other Gospel: Christianity among the World's Religions* (Minneapolis: Fortress Press, 1992).

10. Edward H. Schroeder, "Thursday Theology #21," www.crossings.org (St. Louis: The Crossings Community, 1998).

11. See the recent and quite helpful book by John Sanders, *No Other Name: An Investigation into the Destiny of the Unevangelized* (Grand Rapids: Wm. B. Eerdmans Publishing Co., 1992).

12. WWJD: "What Would Jesus Do."

13. See especially the opening chapters of *The Gospel in a Pluralist Society* (Grand Rapids: Wm. B. Eerdmans Publishing Co., 1989).

14. I mimic Lincoln on purpose. The vast majority of people we preach to devoutly believe that preserving the government of, for, and by the people was well worth the blood shed in the Civil War. How many of these, I wonder, also continue to believe that the martyrs' blood was well shed? Is it not a sign of the pass we have come to that the U.S. system of government is deemed more precious than the Gospel?

15. I have in mind here not scholarly argument but rather the sort of off-hand comment one reasonably expects to hear these days at a mainline pastors' conference. Hence the absence

of documentary citation. For a serious defense of Arius's cause see *When Jesus Became God: the Epic Fight Over Christ's Divinity in the Last Days of Rome* by Richard E. Rubenstein (New York: Harcourt Brace, 1997).

16. On the import of "definition" see chapter 3. Herman Sasse: "Where Christ is, there is the church (*ubi Christus, ibi ecclesia*). The actual presence of Jesus Christ, the exalted Lord, is the secret of the church. It is the ultimate difference between the church and all the religious associations of the world. For this reason the confession that Jesus Christ is Lord is the foundational confession of the church, the confession by which the church stands and falls." ("Jesus Christ is Lord: The Church's Original Confession," in *We Confess Jesus Christ*, trans. Norman Nagel [St. Louis: Concordia Publishing House, 1984] 34).

17. In *The Book of Concord*, trans. and ed. Theodore G. Tappert (Philadelphia: Fortress Press, 1959) 31.

18. In fact owing to his distance, both cultural and geographic, from the third world mother, the pope's role in God's ministry to the toddler is tertiary, even quaternary, the secondary role occupied by the parish priest, or more likely, the village catechist.

19. For a variety of ways in which this manifestation can be both conceptualized and actualized, see Avery Dulles, *Models of the Church*, expanded ed. (New York: Doubleday, Image Books, 1987), especially chaps. 3–6.

Chapter 2:
The Gospel as Proscribed Speech

20. Hauerwas and Willimon, *Resident Aliens*, 124.

21. Along with "the spoken word" (i.e. preaching), baptism, the Sacrament of the Altar, and absolution. See "The Smalcald Articles," Part III, Section IV, in *The Book of Concord*, 310.

22. See Stephen L. Carter, *The Culture of Disbelief: How American Law and Politics Trivialize Religion Devotion* (New

York: BasicBooks, A Division of HarperCollins Publishers, Inc., 1993). Good Lutherans, of course, are deeply trained to be wary of messages from the gut, that font of unruliness, especially when the messages are as sweeping as those I report here. Thus my odd pleasure in having recently observed, at least with respect to the contemporary American situation, a spate of like published testimonies issuing forth from the guts and minds of others better credentialed and undoubtedly more astute than I, Carter being for present purposes the most noteworthy. Carter is an obviously devout Episcopal layman who happens also to be a professor of law at Yale University. This is helpful in taking him seriously—as did the reviewers of the establishment press when this book was published; as did even the President of the United States who was reported to have cited the book in a speech. Carter is neither an angry right wing cleric nor one of their deeply fearful followers. Indeed, assuming the validity of Peter L. Berger's analysis of a *Kulturkampf* between an older business-oriented middle class and a newly arisen knowledge class, Carter's views on the hot button issues of the day tag him clearly as a card-carrying member of the latter. (For Berger's argument see "American Religion: Conservative Upsurge, Liberal Prospects" in *Liberal Protestantism: Realities & Possibilities*, eds. Robert S. Michaelson and Wade Clark Roof [New York: The Pilgrim Press, 1986] 19–36.)

All of which makes it especially telling that Carter's book is from beginning to end a prolonged and deeply rueful reflection on the extent to which the dominant legal and political, culture of the U.S. "presses the religiously faithful to be other than themselves; to act publicly, and *sometimes privately as well* [emphasis added], as though their faith did not matter to them" (3). Writing also from his personal experience as one to whom religious faith and the exercise thereof matters profoundly, he weighs in with an observation closely akin to my own, ". . . for Americans to take their religions seriously, to treat them as ordained rather than chosen, is to risk assignment to the lunatic fringe" (4).

23. See Carter, whose observations make for several highly absorbing and sometimes worrisome hours of reading.

24. See Carter's comment, n. 22.

25. Thus, for example, the otherwise astute Carl E. Braaten: "The occasion for this new struggle [in Western Christian theology] is the impact of religious pluralism on the Christian consciousness. . . . Religious pluralism is like a bomb that has exploded the Christian consciousness." *The Apostolic Imperative: Nature and Aim of the Church's Mission and Ministry* (Minneapolis: Augsburg Publishing House, 1985) 33. Writing with the admirable intent of recalling American Christians, especially those of a Lutheran stripe, to their evangelistic responsibilities, Braaten unfortunately fails—as have so many others—to engage the problem of lost evangelistic nerve at its deepest level.

26. A caveat: the country's multitudinous languages do fall into a greatly smaller number of linguistic families. And whereas one could mount an argument that where there is a distinct language there is also a distinct culture, nonetheless there are sufficient similarities in Papua New Guinean cultures that anthropologists happily group them all under the category "Melanesia," in turn a subcategory of "Oceania." Still, as Papua New Guineans themselves well know, highlanders are not mainline coastal dwellers who are not islanders or swampy Sepik River flatlanders. Nor, in the highlands, are Engas the same as Chimbus, or Chimbus the same as Hagens.

27. For four years in the 1980s, I taught courses in basic biblical literacy at a Papua New Guinean seminary. Again and again I was struck by the way my rudimentary knowledge of local culture and patterns of speech illumined details in biblical stories that had previously been obscure or even meaningless.

28. My sister, Amy E. Burce, Ph.D., a Stanford anthropologist who did her fieldwork in Papua New Guinea, confirms the accuracy of this description.

One small illustration of what I'm talking about here: after four years of inviting seminary students to get the first class of the morning off to a start with a prayer, I finally tumbled to the significance of the line with which each and every one of them invariably began, "We thank you, God our Father, for it was you who woke us up this morning from the sleep of the dead." North American fool that I am, I had always assumed that waking up was something that "simply just happens." I had never thought to give God credit and thanks for the miracle of waking in general, let alone for every specific awakening.

29. See Christopher R. Seitz, "Pluralism and the Lost Art of Christian Apology," *First Things* (June/July 1994) 15–18. Working with the contrast between contemporary America and another highly pluralistic world, i.e., the Mediterranean basin of the first century, Seitz observes rightly that St. Paul encountered no sanctions against religious speech in the open air of the Areopagus (Acts 17:16–33), home of many statues to many gods. Why? Because ". . . in the ancient world, the debate was not whether God existed or could be talked about or related to public actions, but about who God is and what God requires. . . . Some of [the Athenians], it is true, scoff at the notion of the resurrection of the dead—not, however, because they want to keep religious beliefs out of the realm of public discourse, but because, to their minds, it is bad religion" (15).

30. Results from a study conducted under the auspices of the City University of New York. See Richard John Neuhaus, "Pluralism and Wrong Answers," *First Things* (June/July 1994) 72.

31. Meanwhile, the One who sits in the heavens is having the last laugh. Forty years ago the intellectual trendsetters were supremely confident about the impending demise of the transcendent. See Peter L. Berger's citations in *A Rumor of Angels: Modern Society and the Rediscovery of the Supernatural* (New York: Doubleday, 1969; Anchor Books, 1990) 1. In conversation with Berger, by the way, I would propose adding to his so-called "signals of transcendence" (see 59–85) the empiric fact that human beings whether premodern,

modern, or postmodern simply refuse to cease groping for a transcendent dimension. In other words, the unrestrainable impulse to grope is itself a signal that there is something to grope for.

32. This, I think, best accounts for the type of incident recounted by Professor Carter (*The Culture of Disbelief*, 53), in which two Catholic students at Notre Dame Law School were told by classmates that their moral opinion on abortion had no place in a classroom discussion. The roots of their opinion were perceived, quite rightly, as lying in a specifically Catholic telling of spiritual reality. They were invoking, as Carter phrases it, "a forbidden epistemology." But that may be pitching too strongly. "A deeply suspect epistemology" would be more like it—deeply suspect for having to do with the unknowable, and for that reason illegitimate as grounds for suggesting limitations on the behavior of others.

33. Although I don't consciously recall deriving this from Lesslie Newbigin's concept of "Agnostic Pluralism," I dare not suggest a lack of connection between the two (*Truth to Tell*, 56). I am, of course, heavily indebted throughout this present work to Newbigin's analyses, whether of Western cultural presuppositions or of the Gospel's response to these. See further citations *ad hoc*.

34. As Papua New Guineans, I think, have not; so that the optimism of their epistemology might be seen as a psychologically necessary and socially obligatory construction. This would require further discussion, well beyond the scope of my present concerns.

35. For a pithy description of the salient features of postmodernism and their implications for the Church's mission, see Craig Van Gelder, "Postmodernism As An Emerging World View," *Calvin Theological Journal* 26 (November 1991) 412–417.

36. See also Carter, *The Culture of Disbelief*, 23.

Chapter 3:
The Gospel as Required Speech

37. I realize only too well that using this word is akin to handling a vial of nitroglycerine. A thoughtful person, wishing not to be destructive, is obliged to proceed with great care, in full awareness of its explosive potential. I do intend to tread lightly.

38. "The task of the Christian church is to preach Christ and all that pertains to God's eschatological message of salvation that comes solely through Christ" (Braaten, *No Other Gospel,* 132). Thus is churchly purpose described by the theologian who, within the ELCA, has long been leading the effort to debunk the notion that the agnostic imperative of North American culture can somehow be accommodated by an adjustment of the essential Christological content of the Church's faith. See also his "Interreligious Dialogue in the Pluralistic Situation," *dialog* 33 (Fall 1994) 294–8.

39. In keeping with St. Paul's strictures (1 Cor 5:12) I confine my critique to the church I belong to. Let others judge their own households of faith, keeping in mind with me that God judges us all.

40. "Some Other Kind of Soiree," *Forum Letter* 23, no. 2 (18 February 1994) 1. Or again, Braaten and Jensen, *Either Or*, 3. This episode, now six years old, is not yet old enough for its faddish spirit to have crawled back into the woodwork. The shadow lingers.

41. William A. Dyrness, *How Does America Hear the Gospel?* (Grand Rapids: Wm. B. Eerdmans Publishing Co., 1989) 83–105.

42. George Lindbeck, *The Nature of Doctrine: Religion and Theology in a Post-liberal Age* (Philadelphia: The Westminster Press, 1984) 18.

43. Ibid., 32–4.

44. It is no doubt a sign of Lindbeck's own careful dispassion that he "avoids using the word 'heresy,'" speaking rather of times when "rule-doctrines are in 'ineluctable collision'"; for which observation I thank Roger E. Olson, "Whales and Elephants: Both God's Creatures But Can They Meet? Evangelicals and Liberals in Dialogue," *Pro Ecclesia* 4 (Spring 1995) 184 n.

45. Cf. Hauerwas and Willimon: "Faith begins, not in discovery, but in remembrance. . . ." *Resident Aliens*, 52.

46. *Lutheran Book of Worship* (Minneapolis: Augsburg Publishing House, and Philadelphia: Board of Publication, Lutheran Church in America, 1978).

47. G. K. Chesterton, *Orthodoxy: The Romance of Faith* (New York: Doubleday, Image Books, 1959; 2d Image Books ed., 1990) 48.

48. I must add that I agree with Chesterton's wisecrack of 90 years ago that the fashion of assuming that the modern (or postmodern) person *cannot* believe in ancient dogma is "an imbecile habit," if for no other reason than that it persistently ignores, for example, such evidence as the weekly overflowing of cars in the massive parking lots of suburban Roman Catholic churches. Imbecile habits apparently die hard. See *Orthodoxy*, 74.

49. To hear the gurus of church growth tell it, what really matters to the average North American churchgoer (or would-be churchgoer) is not the message but the medium: the pastor's personality, or the warm and friendly "feel" of the church, or the music, or the Sunday School program, or whatever else may happen to appeal to their individual tastes and interests. But are such things *all* that matter? Are people really that superficial?

50. See Carl F. Braaten, *Principles of Lutheran Theology* (Philadelphia: Fortress Press, 1983) 32–9.

51. Randall Balmer, *Mine Eyes Have Seen the Glory: A Journey into the Evangelical Subculture in America* (New York: Oxford University Press, 1989) 204–6.

52. C. S. Lewis makes a compelling argument for common sense in his essay "Modern Theology and Biblical Criticism," in *Christian Reflections* (Grand Rapids: Wm. B. Eerdmans Publishing Co., 1967) 152–66.

53. See also the massive desertion from Jesus after his Bread of Life discourse (John 6).

54. Newbigin, *The Gospel in a Pluralist Society*, 78.

55. Gerhard O. Forde, *Theology is for Proclamation* (Minneapolis: Fortress Press, 1990) 55–6.

56. See 1 Cor 1:21; 2:6–9.

57. Chances are that this was stern old Pastor So-and-So's particular heresy. Derived from a skewed conception of the *sola fide*, this heresy asserts that salvation depends on having one's doctrine straight and firmly swallowed. Odd that this notion should have been so common in the Missouri Synod as I remember it when in fact it was flatly and expressly contradicted by that synod's most revered teacher, founding father C. F. W. Walther. See Thesis XIV in his *The Proper Distinction between Law and Gospel*, (trans. W. H. T. Dau, St. Louis: Concordia Publishing House, 1929) 3.

58. Werner Elert spins out this theme in *The Christian Ethos* (Philadelphia: Fortress Press, 1957) 182–93.

59. "Father, forgive them, for they *know* not what they do" (Luke 23:34). See also the persistent themes in John's Gospel of knowing and not knowing, of light and darkness, of seeing and being blind.

60. See Robert W. Bertram, "Luther on the Unique Mediatorship of Christ," in *The One Mediator, the Saints, and Mary: Lutherans and Catholics in Dialogue VIII*, eds. H. George Anderson, J. Francis Stafford, and Joseph A. Burgess (Minneapolis: Augsburg Fortress, 1992) 249–62. Originally appearing in an in-house seminary publication under the title "How Our Sins Were Christ's," this is the best explication of this theme that I have ever encountered.

61. "My God, my God, *why* have you forsaken me?" (Mark 15:34; Matt 27:46).

62. Luther's explanation of the Third Article in his Small Catechism: "I believe that I cannot by my own understanding or effort believe in Jesus Christ my Lord or come to him. But the Holy Spirit has called me through the Gospel, enlightened me with his gifts, sanctified and kept me in true faith."

63. Newbigin, *The Gospel in a Pluralist Society*, 123–4.

64. For examples see Randall Balmer, *Mine Eyes Have Seen the Glory*, esp. 31–47. For a thoughtful, internal critique of standard evangelical hermeneutics, see Gordon D. Fee, *Gospel and Spirit: Issues in New Testament Hermeneutics* (Peabody, Mass: Hendrickson Publishers, 1991) esp. chaps. 2 and 3.

65. Harrison on herself, "My own theology *is* controversial, and by some standards it *is* heretical." To which I respond: by what conceivable standards is it *not* heretical? See *Making the Connections: Essays in Feminist Social Ethics*, ed. Carol S. Robb (Boston: Beacon Press, 1985) 216.

66. J. Edward Carothers, *The Paralysis of Mainline Protestant Leadership* (Nashville: Abingdon Press, 1990) 118–20. Carothers, it seems to me, represents the logical conclusion of the trend chronicled by Hauerwas and Willimon (*Resident Aliens*, 19–21, in which "modern interpreters of the faith have tended to let the 'modern world' determine the questions and therefore limit the answers").

67. Walter R. Bouman, "Piety in a Secularized Society" in *The Cresset: Occasional Paper 3* (1979) 69. Bertram and Schroeder have devoted much of their energies over the past twenty years to an ongoing exploration of how the Gospel enlivens the workplace. Out of this has evolved a so-called "Crossings Community" which publishes a quarterly newsletter and operates a web site. A growing number of younger theologians are now actively involved in this work. Their product can be sampled and explored at the Crossings web site (www.crossings.org). It appears chiefly in the form of weekly preaching helps and theological essays, typically accessible and highly useful to pastors

who find themselves striving week in and week out to tell the Gospel well.

68. For examples see Braaten, *The Apostolic Imperative*, 41–4; Robert W. Jensen, "The God Wars," in Braaten and Jensen, eds., *Either Or,* 23–36; Hauerwas and Willimon in *Resident Aliens*, 36–43. I must emphasize that I admire these writers greatly and am glad for the courage and passion with which they typically make their excellent arguments.

69. George R. Hunsberger, "Possessing A Peculiar Story: Recovering A Missionary Way of Living," keynote presentation at a consultation of the Gospel and Our Culture Network, 18 February 1993 (copy in present author's files) 6.

Chapter 4:
The Gospel as Promising Proclamation

70. For a brief analysis of American individualism as a product of Puritan theology and Enlightenment philosophy, see Dyrness, 84ff.

71. See Robert Farrar Capon, *Hunting the Divine Fox: An Introduction to the Language of Theology*, reissued in *The Romance of the Word: One Man's Love Affair with Theology* (Grand Rapids: Wm. B. Eerdmans Publishing Co., 1995) 270–6. In the latter part of this paragraph, I have blended Capon with Luther. I am confident that both would approve.

72. James Arne Nestingen, *Authority and Resistance in the ELCA* (www.wordalone.org/nestingen.htm, 2000). Nestingen's comment, contrasting Gospel with law as categories of speech, bears quoting in full: "The gospel is performative—precisely in, with, and under all the other human words, it does what it says, carrying the hearer beyond alternatives as it actually creates faith, bestows freedom, engenders joy, finally raises the dead. Such claims can be made for the gospel because of the Spirit who animates it."

References Cited

Balmer, Randall. 1989. *Mine Eyes Have Seen the Glory: A Journey into the Evangelical Subculture in America.* New York: Oxford University Press.

Becker, May Lamberton. 1946. "How This Book Came to be Written." Introduction to *Pride and Prejudice* by Jane Austen. Cleveland and New York: The World Publishing Company.

Berger, Peter L. 1986. "American Religion: Conservative Upsurge, Liberal Prospects." In *Liberal Protestantism: Realities & Possibilities*, Eds. Robert S. Michaelson and Wade Clark Roof, 19–36. New York: The Pilgrim Press.

——. 1969. *A Rumor of Angels: Modern Society and the Rediscovery of the Supernatural.* New York: Doubleday; Anchor Books, 1990.

Bertram, Robert W. 1992. "Luther on the Unique Mediatorship of Christ." In *The One Mediator, the Saints, and Mary: Lutherans and Catholics in Dialogue VIII.* Eds. H. George Anderson, J. Francis Stafford, and Joseph A. Burgess, 249–62. Minneapolis: Augsburg Fortress.

The Book of Concord. 1959. Trans. and ed. by Theodore G. Tappert. Philadelphia: Fortress Press.

Bouman, Walter R. "Piety in a Secularized Society." In *The Cresset: Occasional Paper* 3, 1979: 64–75.

Braaten, Carl E. and Robert W. Jenson, eds. 1995. *Either Or: The Gospel or Neopaganism*. Grand Rapids: William B. Eerdmans Publishing Company.

Braaten, Carl E. 1994. "Interreligious Dialogue in the Pluralistic Situation." *dialog* 33 294–8.

——. 1992. *No Other Gospel: Christianity among the World's Religions*. Minneapolis: Fortress Press.

——. 1985. *The Apostolic Imperative: Nature and Aim of the Church's Mission and Ministry*. Minneapolis: Augsburg Publishing House.

——. 1983. *Principles of Lutheran Theology*. Philadelphia: Fortress Press.

Capon, Robert Farrar. 1995. *The Romance of the Word: One Man's Love Affair with Theology*. Grand Rapids: Wm. B. Eerdmans Publishing Co.

Carothers, J. Edward. 1990. *The Paralysis of Mainline Protestant Leadership*. Nashville: Abingdon Press.

Carter, Stephen L. 1993. *The Culture of Disbelief: How American Law and Politics Trivialize Religion Devotion*. New York: BasicBooks, A Division of HarperCollins Publishers, Inc.

Chesterton, G. K. 1990. *Orthodoxy: The Romance of Faith*. New York: Doubleday, Image Books, 1959, 2d Image Books edition.

Cox, Harvey. 1999. "The Market as God: Living in the New Dispensation." In *Atlantic* 283 18–23.

——. 1965. *The Secular City: Secularization and Urbanization in Theological Perspective*. New York: The Macmillan Company.

Dulles, Avery. 1987. *Models of the Church*. Expanded ed. New York: Doubleday, Image Books.

Dyrness, William A. 1989. *How Does America Hear the Gospel?* Grand Rapids: Wm. B. Eerdmans Publishing Co.

Elert, Werner. 1957. *The Christian Ethos*. Philadelphia: Fortress Press.

Fee, Gordon D. 1991. *Gospel and Spirit: Issues in New Testament Hermeneutics*. Peabody, Mass: Hendrickson Publishers.

Forde, Gerhard O. 1990. *Theology is for Proclamation*. Minneapolis: Fortress Press.

Fukuyama, Francis. 1999. "The Great Disruption: Human Nature and the Reconstitution of Social Order." *Atlantic* 283 55–80.

Gilkey, Langdon. 1969. *Naming the Whirlwind: The Renewal of God-Language*. Indianapolis: The Bobbs-Merrill Co., Inc.

Hall, Douglas John. 1997. *The End of Christendom and the Future of Christianity*. Christian Mission and Modern Culture Series. Harrisburg, Penn: Trinity Press International.

Harrison, Beverly Wildung. 1985. *Making the Connections: Essays in Feminist Social Ethics*. Ed. by Carol S. Robb. Boston: Beacon Press.

Hauerwas, Stanley and William H. Willimon. 1989. *Resident Aliens: Life in the Christian Colony*. Nashville: Abingdon Press.

Hunsberger,George R. 1993. "Possessing A Peculiar Story: Recovering A Missionary Way of Living." Keynote presentation at a consultation of the Gospel and Our Culture Network.

Lewis, C. S. 1967. *Christian Reflections*. Grand Rapids: Wm. B. Eerdmans Publishing Co.

Lindbeck, George A. 1984. *The Nature of Doctrine: Religion and Theology in a Post-liberal Age*. Philadelphia: The Westminster Press.

Nestingen, James Arne. 2000. *Authority and Resistance in the ELCA*. Online. Internet; www.wordalone.org/nestingen.htm.

Neuhaus, Richard John. 1994. "Pluralism and Wrong Answers." *First Things*, no. 44 72–3.

——. 1984. *The Naked Public Square: Religion and Democracy in America*. Grand Rapids: Wm. B. Eerdmans Publishing Co.

Newbigin, Lesslie. 1991. *Truth To Tell*. Grand Rapids: Wm. B. Eerdmans Publishing Co.

——. 1989. *The Gospel in a Pluralist Society*. Grand Rapids: Wm. B. Eerdmans Publishing Co.

Niebuhr, H. Richard. 1951. *Christ and Culture*. New York: Harper & Brothers; Harper Torchbooks, 1956.

Olson, Roger E. 1995. "Whales and Elephants: Both God's Creatures But Can They Meet? Evangelicals and Liberals in Dialogue." *Pro Ecclesia* 4 165–89.

Sanders, John. 1992. *No Other Name: An Investigation into the Destiny of the Unevangelized*. Grand Rapids: Wm. B. Eerdmans Publishing Co.

Sasse, Hermann. 1984. *We Confess Jesus Christ*. Trans. Norman Nagel. St. Louis: Concordia Publishing House.

Schroeder, Edward H. 1998. "Thursday Theology #21." At www.crossings.org. St Louis: The Crossings Community.

Seitz, Christopher R. 1994. "Pluralism and the Lost Art of Christian Apology." *First Things*, no. 44 15–8.

Van Gelder, Craig. 1991. "Postmodernism As An Emerging World View." *Calvin Theological Journal* 26 412–7.

Walther, C. F. W. 1929. *The Proper Distinction between Law and Gospel*. Trans. W. H. T. Dau. St. Louis: Concordia Publishing House.